Leeds Minster

LEEDS MINSTER

Edited by Christopher Webster

Proceedings of the
Ecclesiological Society Conference,
Leeds, September 2021

ISBN: 978-0-946823-27-7
ISSN: 1460-4213

Published 2022 by the Ecclesiological Society
c/o The Society of Antiquaries of London
Burlington House
Piccadilly
London
W1V 0HS

The Ecclesiological Society is a registered charity. Charity no. 210501.
Join the society at: www.ecclsoc.org

The views expressed in this publication are those of the authors and do not necessarily represent those of the Ecclesiological Society or its officers.

Designed by Vera Fabiankova
Printed in the UK by Henry Ling Ltd, at the Dorset Press, Dorchester, DT1 1HD

Cover image: Leeds Parish Church from the north-west. (Christopher Webster)
Frontispiece: Leeds Parish Church, view looking east. (Engraving after a drawing by W. Richardson, published 1841)

LEEDS MINSTER

Contributors

JANET DOUGLAS was formerly a lecturer in Politics at Leeds Beckett University and for 40 years has been a member of the West Yorkshire Group of the Victorian Society. She is the author of a wide range of publications on aspects of the history of Leeds, her most recent published contributions are 'Women, Reading and the Leeds Library' which appeared in *Through these Pages: 250 Years of the Leeds Library*, and 'Zionism in Leeds 1892–1939' in *Leeds and its Jewish Community*.

DR KEVIN GRADY was a lecturer in Economic History at Exeter and Leeds Universities before becoming Director of Leeds Civic Trust. He has written extensively on the history of Leeds and the West Riding.

DR CHRISTOPHER HAMMOND is a member of the Northern Buildings Committee of the Victorian Society and was formerly Conservation Secretary of the West Yorkshire Group. He served, as the National Amenity Societies' representative, on the former Bradford DAC and latterly the Leeds (Anglican) DAC.

DR SIMON LINDLEY came from St Albans Cathedral to Leeds in 1975 to succeed Donald Hunt at what was then the Parish Church and subsequently, in 1976, followed him in addition as City Organist at Leeds Town Hall. He also served as founder Music Director of the St Peter's Singers, established by Harry Fearnley in 1997.

KENNETH POWELL is an architectural critic and historian based in London and Leeds. He is a member of the London Diocesan Advisory Committee.

MICHAEL SWIFT's dissertation for his Master's degree for Trinity & All Saints, University of Leeds, 1999, was on the development of stained-glass windows in the Anglican churches of Leeds, 1841–60. For twenty years he has been the stained glass advisor for the Diocese of Truro and for Truro Cathedral, publishing many articles in journals and on his website www.cornishstainedglass.org.

DR CHRISTOPHER WEBSTER is an architectural historian and a Research Associate at the University of York. He has published widely on the late-Georgian and early-Victorian periods in England, focusing on the design of Anglican churches, the period's stylistic debates and the development of the architectural profession.

ALEXANDER WOODROW is the Organist and Director of Music at Leeds Minster, having served previously in a similar capacity at Bradford Cathedral. In addition, he is Director of Music of the St Peter's Singers of Leeds and a prominent organ recitalist throughout the UK.

Preface

On 2 September 1841 the new parish church of Leeds was consecrated. The service was performed by the Bishop of Ripon, in the presence of the Archbishop of York and he was accompanied by two other bishops. Also there were between 280 and 400 clergy, depending on which account one reads,[1] who came from 'every diocese in the country' (see Fig. 3.4). And there were 3,000 invited guests. It was, by all accounts, a memorable occasion.[2] However, it was significant not just for the parishioners in Leeds. It is not unreasonable to conclude it was an event of almost unparalleled importance for the national Church, then struggling to make itself relevant for the modern, industrial age.

Here was the largest new church erected in England since St Paul's in London and 'as grand as any cathedral', according to Owen Chadwick.[3] Indeed, the *Church of England Magazine* concluded 'The church is one of the noblest in the kingdom'.[4] However, its importance was not just its size and its commanding design. Also of fundamental significance were the messages the building was expected to generate. Chantrell very successfully interpreted Hook's ambitions to have a church that would impress – a 'standing sermon', to quote Hook – and remind worshippers of the visual as well as the spiritual comforts inherent in the Established Church.[5] And while it was, indeed, the *Reformed* Church, the Gothic design was a confident statement and a reminder of a distant, but meaningful, Anglican heritage. In Hook's drive to win back those who had deserted the Church for Nonconformity, it was a powerful message.

Equally important were the liturgical innovations that Hook introduced. The opening of the new church represented one of the key moments in the move towards the internal arrangement that would soon become almost ubiquitous across the Anglican world. Indeed, the preacher at the consecration was George Washington Doane, Bishop of New Jersey, who made the 3,000 mile journey across the Atlantic to deliver the sermon and learn more about the vicar's liturgical thinking, enthusiastic to introduce new ideas in the United States. But Hook was not just an idealistic liturgical innovator: he was also a man of great vision, ambition and energy, 'the greatest parish priest of the nineteenth century', according to James Rusby.[6]

We need to remember that through the late-Georgian period, the Church of England occupied a decidedly precarious position. While it was, indeed, the *Established* Church, it was under a significant threat due to the growth of Nonconformity and Roman Catholicism, and equally challenging was the spread of atheism. The problem was most pronounced in large, rapidly expanding industrial, urban centres in the north of England, like Leeds.

Thus in Leeds, in 1841, came together all the crucial ingredients in the longed-for Anglican revival: a magnificent new building, a charismatic and energetic cleric, and a parish ripe for regeneration. The eyes of the Anglican world were, indeed, focused on Leeds. Later in the nineteenth century, Leeds was, not unreasonably, referred to as 'the model parish of England'.[7]

These themes were explored in the papers delivered at the 2021 conference and published here.

It is believed the first church on this site was built more than a thousand years ago and over the years has had a number of designations. Throughout the nineteenth and twentieth centuries it was generally referred to as Leeds Parish Church; occasionally as St Peter-at-Leeds. In 2012 it was given the honorific title of Leeds Minster. During the period covered by the papers in this publication, it was consistently referred to as Leeds Parish Church and to avoid any confusion, this designation is used throughout this publication.

I am deeply grateful to the authors who have shared their considerable scholarship and research in the papers that follow. Although aspects of the church and Dr Hook's endeavours are reasonably well known,[8] there is much new material on both while other papers examine subjects deserving re-examination, for instance the 'old' parish church, the composition of the congregation, Hook's concept of an appropriate liturgy and his remarkable endeavours to strengthen the Established Church in his huge parish. I am grateful to Dr Roy Yates who has generously shared his considerable research with several of the contributors. Thanks are due to Mark Kirby, the Ecclesiological Society's Chair, who did a commendable job of taking questions throughout the day, editing them and putting them to the speakers.

The conference was conceived in mid-2019, well before most people had even envisaged Covid, Zoom and Eventbrite. It was going to be a conventional, traditional conference where like-minded folk assembled to hear the papers, after posting their cheques! By 2021, administration of the conference generated challenges beyond anything I could ever have imagined two years earlier. Indeed, the event would have been impossible without the assistance of numerous specialists who volunteered to take on demanding roles: Robert Andrews who was Conference Administrator and, among many tasks, performed a commendable job with the publicity and general organisation; Graham West who devoted several days to overseeing the various technical challenges inherent in a conference available on Zoom as well as 'in the room'; and Becky Payne who assisted in various ways, most notably with the booking arrangements. I am grateful to Geoff Brandwood who volunteered to station himself at the door to check tickets and to Susan Webster who willingly took the role of general factotum.

I would like to record my thanks to the staff at Leeds Minster: the Rector, Canon Sam Corley – now Bishop of Stockport – was an enthusiastic supporter of this project; and Richard Butterfield, the Minster's Director of Operations, provided significant assistance on a range of fronts. Iain Howell, the Minster Caretaker, provided valuable support, especially with technical issues. I am also grateful to Rhoda Wallace and Trevor Parker, the Churchwardens, for help in various ways.

Finally, I would like to thank Martin Hamilton, Director of the Leeds Civic Trust, and Christopher Hutton, Chair of the Grants Committee of Leeds Philosophical and Literary Society, for generous grants to support this publication.

Christopher Webster

Notes

1. The most reliable list appeared in Anon., *The Seven Sermons Preached at the Consecration and Reopening of the Parish Church of Leeds* (Leeds, 1841), lxv-lxxxvi. This includes 300 names, but the compiler acknowledges that while his list was 'as correct … as can be given … there were many Clergymen present whose names were unknown', lxv.
2. John Mayhall, *Annals of Leeds*, (Leeds, 1862), vol 1, 472.
3. Owen Chadwick, *The Victorian Church* (London, 1971), pt 1, 413.
4. *Church of England Magazine*, 11, 1841, 'Register of Ecclesiastical Intelligence', October 1841, 28.
5. *Leeds Intelligencer*, 11 November 1837.
6. James Rusby, *History of Leeds Parish Church* (Leeds, 1896), 66.
7. David Thornton, *Leeds: a Biographical Dictionary* (Leeds, 2021), p. 136.
8. Those seeking more about Hook's work in Leeds are directed to H. W. Dalton, 'Walter Farquhar Hook, Vicar of Leeds' (*Publications of the Thoresby Society*, Leeds, 1990); H. W. Dalton, 'Anglican Resurgence under W. F. Hook in Early Victorian Leeds' (Publications of the Thoresby Society, hereafter PTS, Leeds, 2002).

1.

The Medieval Parish Church of Leeds

KEVIN GRADY

In 2012 Leeds Parish Church was renamed Leeds Minster, though for many it will forever be thought of as the 'Parish Church'. Opened in 1841, the present-day church, designed by R. D. Chantrell, replaced a building with a rich history both in its associations and its architectural form. Indeed, to fully understsand the decisions made by Chantrell and Hook in conceiving their new church, one has to understand the building it replaced. Unlike many Yorkshire towns and villages, Leeds does not have its medieval parish church to provide a physical embodiment of the development of the place, and a direct connection with the people about whom we read in documents. This paper discusses the physical development of what in all probability were four churches which successively occupied the site between the seventh century and 1838, and seeks to recreate in the reader's mind the medieval church before its demolition. It is accompanied by all the known images of the medieval building, most notably a remarkable set of watercolours by Joseph and John Rhodes (father and son) painted on the eve of its demolition; they are reproduced here in their entirety for the first time.

Leeds' first and second churches

The name 'Leeds' is derived from the British word 'Loidis', the name given to a region of the ancient British kingdom of Elmet, and ultimately to a single important place within it. Indeed Leeds, today a great city within the metropolitan county of West Yorkshire, may have been the last independent capital of Elmet before it was overwhelmed by the advancing Anglo-Saxons early in the seventh century. It is located on a strategic river crossing point where the narrow Aire valley, at the eastern edge of the Pennines, opens on to the broad lowlands of the Vale of York. The valley was a natural east to west route-way across the Pennines much used in ancient times. A second route to Leeds crossed the mountain range from the south-west via Standedge where the Pennines are at their narrowest. The convergence of the two routes where the River Aire could be relatively easily forded made Leeds a natural site for settlement, and it was established on an area of well-drained land where the village's first medieval street, today known as Kirkgate, was created. It also became a much travelled through place on the route from York to Ireland.[1]

The British kingdom of Elmet was conquered by Edwin, the Anglo-Saxon king of Northumbria, soon after 617. In the year 625 AD, the monk Paulinus became chaplain to Princess Ethelburga of Kent. When she married Edwin, he too became a Christian and actively promoted his new faith. The Venerable Bede, writing around 730 AD, recorded in his *Ecclesiastical History of the English Nation* that after Edwin conquered the kingdom of Elmet: 'A church was built in the royal country-seat of Campodunum, but this, together with all the other buildings, was burned by the pagans [Penda, the Anglo Saxon king of Mercia] who killed king Edwin [in 633] and later kings replaced this by another in the vicinity of Loidis.' Some historians have suggested that this church may have been on the site of Leeds Minster.[2]

Regardless of conjecture on this point, it is clear that there was a very early church in Leeds and it flourished. The compelling evidence for this is that, during the demolition of the medieval parish church which commenced in March 1838, the remains of five early tenth-century Anglo-Danish crosses were found in the rubble of the church tower (Fig. 1.1). The most complete of them stands today within Leeds Minster to the right of the altar.[3] Therefore, by the early tenth century, Leeds and its church were of sufficient importance for Danish noblemen to choose to be buried there. The Danes had begun to settle in the Leeds area around 871 (the year Alfred the Great became King of Wessex). The crosses suggest by their number and ornateness that Leeds, with its strategic location, was the site of one of three major minster churches in this area of Yorkshire, each set in a major river valley, the other two being at Dewsbury in the Calder valley and Otley in the Wharfe valley (Fig. 1.1).[4]

The large parish of Leeds as it emerged in the later Middle Ages comprised not only the manor of Leeds but also the neighbouring manors of Allerton, Gipton, Osmondthorpe, Beeston, Hunslet, Holbeck, Wortley, Bramley, Armley and Headingley; in all an area of thirty-two square miles. Historic geographers have suggested that the land contained within the parish had once been one large British estate, and that perhaps as first Anglo-Saxons and then Scandinavian settlers occupied the area, this estate was subdivided into lesser estates served by the mother church in Leeds (Fig. 1.2).[5]

Soon after invading England in 1066, William the Conqueror gave the manor of 'Leedes', and many other estates, to one of his powerful Norman barons, Ilbert de Lacy. Domesday Book in 1086 records a church and a priest in the manor of Leeds. Shortly after 1086, Ilbert

Fig. 1.1: Reconstruction painting of early tenth-century crosses found in the rubble of the Parish Church tower in 1838. (© Peter Brears)

granted the manor of Leeds to another wealthy Norman baron, Ralph Paynel.[6] And three years later, in 1089, Ralph, as an act of piety, granted the church and its income, plus the surrounding village, to the Benedictine priory of Holy Trinity in York, which he had founded or re-endowed. This was a French order of monks, whose mother house was at Marmoutier in northern France. Men like Ralph Paynel founded priories and chantries not only as acts of religious piety, but also as an insurance policy – the charter of Holy Trinity Priory specifically states that the monks should pray for the soul of their founder and his family.[7] In addition to the Parish Church and its income, Ralph's gift included the village immediately around the church, 'the tithe of the hall', and income from lands in the adjacent manor of Holbeck. Subsequently, these lands, property and income were known as the rectory manor of Leeds Kirkgate-cum-Holbeck.

Fig. 1.2: Reconstruction painting of the Leeds manor house (left) and the church in ditched enclosures in 1089. (© Peter Brears)

Fig. 1.2 shows part of a reconstruction painting of the village of Leeds *c.*1089 with the moated enclosures of Leeds manor house and the church. The protection of the church by a surrounding ditch is confirmed by an account of a brawl at the church in 1320, but what is open to conjecture is the size of the church around the time of the Norman Conquest.[8] Though the church seemingly had only one priest by the time of Domesday Book, it may well have been considerably larger than the illustration suggests. The most prominent feature of the medieval church as it appears in engravings dating from the late seventeenth and early eighteenth centuries is its large central tower. This feature is extremely unusual in a post-Conquest church; almost no central-tower churches were built after the third quarter of the twelfth century. Even if the surviving fabric of a central-tower church is later, its form is almost always an artefact of a pre-Conquest church with a central tower or raised area at the east of the nave, with north, south and east porticus (which evolved into transepts or the east end of wide nave aisles) and the nave to the west. The plan form of the medieval St Peter's therefore supports the suggestion made earlier that before the Conquest it had been a substantial minster church with a significant religious community.[9]

The third church

The monks and founders of Holy Trinity were keen to protect their asset in Leeds. Around 1119 another charter was obtained from the Paynel family confirming Ralph's gift, together with additional donations made by their vassals and other benefactors. It also forbade anyone, including hermits, from building a chapel or any kind of oratory within the bounds of the parish without the permission of the Prior and Convent, and decreed that no one else was to minister to the parishioners of Leeds or receive their benefactions.[10] The Priory had presented a vicar to the church to minister to the spiritual needs of the parish; one-third of the church's income was received by the vicar; and two-thirds by the priory.

The church in Leeds was either enlarged or substantially rebuilt relatively soon after the monks acquired it, somewhere between 1089 and 1120, creating what might be regarded as the third church on the site. Major Moore (the assistant architect during the demolition and rebuilding of the Parish Church in 1838) had no doubt that there had been a 'third church' built on the site about the end of the eleventh and commencement of the twelfth century, noting that many fragments of 'Early Norman work' had been found during the demolition – the charring of some proving that it had later for the most part been destroyed by fire.[11] Fenteman's *Guide to Leeds* published in 1858 confirmed this, noting that during the demolition work in 1838, apart from the stone crosses, 'the most ancient fragments discovered were of the Norman Church of Leeds; not the one mentioned in the Domesday Survey, but the church renewed about the latter end of the eleventh or commencement of the twelfth century.'[12] Clearly, not all these remains were below ground because Ralph Thoresby, the Leeds antiquarian (1658–1725), observed that in his day 'some parts of the church might be said to be of that antiquity' though the ancient church was chiefly of the Perpendicular period.[13] Sadly, no illustrations showing this early Norman work survive.

The fourth church

The fire which severely damaged the third church precipitated the substantial rebuilding of the Parish Church during the fourteenth century creating the 'fourth church'.[14] The monks of Holy Trinity Priory had prospered as had Leeds and its parish, its population growing significantly. Briggate, the long broad street with its sixty burgage plots, laid out as the principal feature of the manorial borough created by Maurice Paynel in 1207, had become an important market centre. Two fulling mills had been erected close to Leeds Bridge in 1322 and 1356 respectively to serve the town's substantial community of woollen cloth workers. The monks (represented by a vicar in Leeds) had rebuilt the church in an impressive manner during the reign of Edward III, 1327–77. Evidence of the style of that period still remained in the eighteenth century. Rusby, the Victorian historian of the church, wrote in 1898: 'The main features of the church belonged to the Perpendicular Period. Its shape was that of a cross with choir, transepts, nave aisles and a tower 96 feet high above the crossing.'[15] It was one of the largest parish churches in the West Riding, reflecting the importance of the settlement (see Figs 1.3 and 1.4).

The church was then enlarged at the end of the fifteenth/very early sixteenth century, in the reign of Henry VII or early part of the reign of Henry VIII. When the church was demolished in 1838 and its floor excavated, a considerable quantity of molten lead, mixed with charred wood, broken stone and glass was found about a foot and a half below the floor of the chancel, revealing that the chancel at least had been destroyed by fire c.1500, and had been rebuilt.[16] The evidence of architectural style showed that the chancel section of the south aisle had been rebuilt in the Tudor period and an outer north aisle had been added around the same time. Thus, the church reached its pre-demolition 1838 size in the Tudor period.

Fig. 1.3: The South Prospect of St Peter's Church at Leeds. (By Francis Place in R. Thoresby, *Ducatus Leodiensis* (1715))

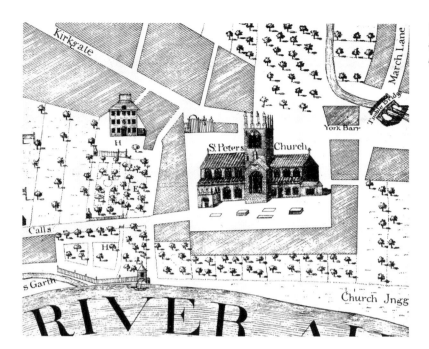

Fig. 1.4: The Parish Church shown on John Cossins', *New & Exact Plan of the Town of Leedes*, 1726.

Corporation of London surveyors visiting Leeds in 1628 to survey the manor – which the cash-strapped Charles I had just sold to the Corporation – observed that: 'The Church of Leeds (which is a verie faire church built after a cathedrall structure and having one side thereof double Iled) is soe besett with scaffold over scaffold [wooden galleries] so as noe place is voide to heare ye Minister'[17] (Fig. 1.5).

In summary, as the Figures 1.3, 1.4 and 1.5 show, by the early seventeenth century the church consisted of a nave plus three aisles, and a crossing supporting a 96-foot high central tower, with transepts on either side, beyond which was an enormous 'quire' or chancel four aisles wide, with the altar at its east end. Though Kirkgate on the north side of the church was the principal thoroughfare west to east in the later Middle Ages, John Cossins' town plan of 1726 (Fig. 1.4) shows the church effectively faced south; its entry by a porch on that side reflected the earlier importance of The Calls, the trackway running close to the riverbank from Leeds Bridge ultimately running in the direction of York.

Francis Place's *South Prospect of St Peter's* drawn in 1715 (Fig. 1.3) highlights the striking contrast between square-headed 'Tudor' windows of the south aisle at the chancel or quire end, with the pointed-headed windows at its west end. The vignette on Cossins' plan seemingly exaggerates the size of the clerestory windows, which no doubt are more accurately depicted as quite small on Place's *Prospect*. Joseph Rhodes' *c*.1838 painting of the north-west side of the church (Fig. 1.6) – the only

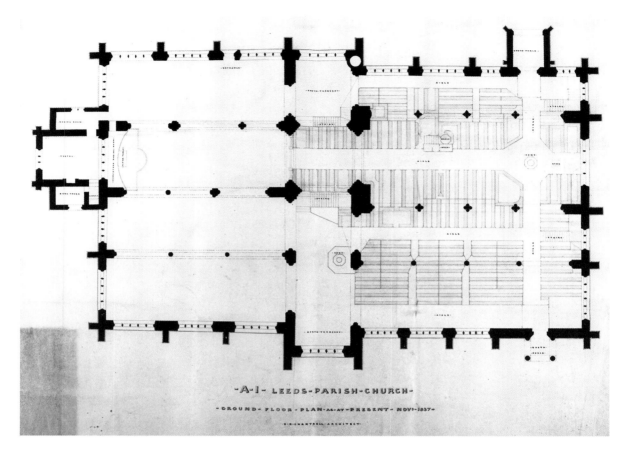

Fig. 1.5: Ground Plan of the medieval church in November 1837 before demolition, drawn by R. D. Chantrell. South is at the top of the picture. (Borthwick Institute)

surviving image of the north side of the church – allows us to see clearly its twin aisles. The outer north aisle has square-headed windows, while the west gable end of the inner aisle has a large pointed-headed window, as does the end of the north transept.

Leeds needed a large parish church. Even though by the seventeenth century there were six chapels serving the out-townships of the parish, the church was too small for its congregation. A complaint to the Court of Chancery in 1615 highlighted this inadequacy, pointing out that the town and parish consisted of over five thousand worshippers; though many lived three or four miles from the church, three or four thousand usually attended its services on Sundays. A partial solution came in 1634 when the town gained a second Anglican church, St John's, New Briggate.[18]

Chapels and chantries

We can gain only glimpses of the character of the interior of the church in the century or so before the Reformation. Evidently, it had a considerable amount of stained glass; Major Moore noted that, during the demolition, a large quantity of stained and painted glass of an early date was found which had been used to pack the courses of stones, 'some of very perfect colour, particularly the ruby'. Indeed, the church must have been colourful; Moore also recalled that some excellent remains of 'fresco paintings' were found on the walls, underneath many coats of colouring and whitewash.[19]

An important feature of the pre-Reformation church had been its chapels, of which there had been at least six within the building. Thoresby in 1715 noted the remaining physical evidence of them and their designations where he could discern them. It seems likely that they were principally located in the chancel. Thoresby observed that:

> This spacious Quire was in the Days of Darkness canton'd into many distinct Cells or Chapels by several Walls, as is evident in the Breaches in the Capitals and Pedestals of the Pillars. At the East End [there] were three, besides the High Altar; but how many upon the North and South Sides [of the Quire], I cannot distinctly tell. … The Partition Walls were broken down in St. Paul's by Bishop Riley, Anno 1550; but when in these Northern Parts has not yet occurred to me, probably at the same Time when the Images were removed, the Acroters, or protruberent Stones upon which they placed those Blind Maummets [statues of saints] are yet [i.e. still] to be seen.

He identified the position of the chapel dedicated to the Blessed Virgin Mary (or the 'Lady's Service') as being in the north-east corner of the Quire from 'the Monogram under a Crown wrought in the Stone-work of the Church's Wall, and a Female crowned Head in the Window'; the chapel of the Jesu Guild he identified as being in its south-east corner

Fig. 1.6: Parish Church north-west view, c.1838 by Joseph Rhodes. (By kind permission of Leeds Libraries, www.leodis.net)

by 'the ancient Character for Jesus ihc being cut in the Wood-work of the Roof, and painted in the Window; where also remains the Picture of our Saviour's Head crowned with Thornes.' But he could not identify the positions in the church of 'the particular Chancels of St. Trinity, St. Mary's [Magdalene] and the Rockley Wheare [Quire] mentioned in ancient writings.' St Katherine's Chapel, however, he was certain had been in the south transept, 'where the Place for Holy-Water is yet to be seen.'[20]

Three at least of these were chantry chapels with endowments which endured until the dissolution of the chantries under the Acts of 1545 and 1547.[21] The chapel of St Mary Magdalen had been founded in 1470 by William Evers, Vicar of Leeds, to pray for the soul of the founder and all Christian souls. At the time of the dissolution, Thomas Jeffrayson was incumbent, and was charged to serve at the altar of the chapel and to assist at the high altar at divine worship, holydays and festivals.[22]

Most is known about St Katherine's chapel which had been founded by Thomas Clarell in 1489, when he was vicar, to pray for the souls of King Edward IV and Queen Elizabeth, the founder's soul, and all Christian souls. Clarell was also remembered for decorating the church with new pictures; perhaps these were some of the frescoes noted by Major Moore. Clarell's endowment and subsequent bequests provided for a house in Kirkgate for the chantry priest, which had a 'hospital' or almshouses next to it. The most notable of its priests was William Sheaffield who it seems probably ran a school as part of his duties as a chantry priest, and through a bequest in his will of 1552 is believed to have founded and endowed Leeds Grammar School.[23]

The chapel of the Blessed Virgin Mary (or Lady Chapel) also was a chantry. The Chantry Certificates of 1545 suggest that there were *two* chantries of Our Lady in the Parish Church, and their incumbents were John Mathew and Robert Fell, whose duties also included ministering in the quire as assistants to the vicar. Both received pensions at the dissolution of the chantries. Rather than there being two Lady Chapels, it seems more likely that the Lady Chapel had two separate endowments for chantry priests.[24]

Prayers for the dead could be offered in any of the chapels in the church irrespective of whether they had chantry endowments. The chapel of the Leeds Jesus Guild, which had existed since at least 1388, was funded by the guild to support a chaplain to offer masses for the souls of guild members. The guild was still in existence in the 1530s, but does not figure in the chantry survey of 1545; it seems likely that it went into liquidation in anticipation of the dissolution.

On the eve of the dissolution of the monasteries the life of the Parish Church must have been very active with a considerable number of priests. A clerical subsidy, which though not dated, falls between 1521 and 1539, gives the names of no less than seven priests described as 'chaplains of Leeds', meaning that they were attached to the high altar and were not chantry priests. Added to the vicar, William Eure, and the four or five chantry priests, this made a clerical complement of at least twelve.[25] At the Dissolution, Holy Trinity Priory was surrendered to the Crown with all its property, rights and privileges. Holy Trinity's share of the parish tithes were appropriated to Christ Church College, Oxford, while the vicar's tithes appear to have been left untouched. The advowson of St Peter's (the right to appoint the vicar) was granted to Thomas Culpepper, gentleman of London; but in 1588 some leading townsmen purchased the advowson on behalf of the parishioners.[26]

The Parish Church in Ralph Thoresby's day

We are fortunate through Ralph Thoresby's writings, *Ducatus Leodiensis* (1715) and *Vicaria Leodiensis* (1724), to have an excellent description of the Parish Church in the early eighteenth century, and the adornment of it between 1710 and 1724. The important series of watercolour sketches of the church made by Joseph and John Rhodes around 1838 on the eve of the church's demolition provide a wonderful accompaniment to Thoresby's description. The Rhodes were Leeds artists of some distinction – John in particular gained a national reputation – their paintings of the church were merely hurriedly produced sketches.[27] While following Thoresby's description and the Rhodes' paintings, it is helpful to bear in mind that the new Parish Church of 1838–41 – today's Minster – was rebuilt on exactly the same footprint as the medieval Parish Church.[28]

In the main body of *Ducatus* Thoresby guides us around the church, describing its form, furnishings and monuments, a description to which he adds, with pride and considerable excitement, new detail in an addendum, the need for which arose in part from the considerable improvements made to the church in the three or four years while his book was in the process of publication. These improvements were superintended by Thoresby's friend and churchwarden, the dynamic William Cookson, the wealthy cloth merchant and alderman of Leeds Corporation whose fine house, with its beautiful garden extending down to the river, can be seen to the left of the churchyard on Cossins' Plan (Fig. 1.4). Thoresby begins his description with considerable gravitas:

The parish church (which was dedicated to St Peter) is a very spacious and strong Fabrick, an Emblem of the Church Militant, black, but comely, being of great Antiquity; it doth not pretend to the Mode of reformed Architecture, but is strong and useful. ... It is evidently the Work of several Ages; which have added both to its Length, Breadth and Height. The Fabric of this [church] is plain but venerable; the Walls wholly of Free-stone, the Roof entirely cover'd with Lead, except part of the Quire. ... It is built after the Manner of a Cathedral, with a large cross Isle, and the Steeple or Tower in the middle of it. The Dimensions of the Church are, Length 165 foot, Breadth 97; Height of the Nave of the Church 51, and of the Steeple 96.[29]

Proud of Leeds and ever keen to boost its reputation, he declared that 'Whoever shall compare these [its dimensions] with those churches in the *New View of London* (1709) will find there are but two in the 106 there mention'd (except the Cathedrals of St Paul's and Westminster) that exceed it in length, ... and as to breadth there is but one that equals it and but one that surmounts it in height in the body of the church.'

The layout of the medieval building is illustrated by the ground plan drawn in November 1837 by Dennis Chantrell when he was commissioned initially to renovate and modify the church (Fig. 1.5).

The nave

Moving on to the interior, Thoresby first described the nave (Fig. 1.7).

In the Nave of the Church are four Isles (which is one more than usual) that run from the cross Isle to the West End, where is a stately Font; 'tis gilt and painted, and stands upon an Ascent of three Steps, surrounded with Rails and Banisters.[30] Upon the North and East are spacious Galleries of Wainscot, wrought with [a] Variety of Work, directly opposite to the Pulpit, which is adorned with a Black Velvet Cloth and Gold Fringe, are the Town's Arms, betwixt two gilt maces in relieve. ... The whole is surrounded with a Garter, inscribed *Sigillum Burgi de Leedes, 1660.*

He noted that 'the Body of the Church [by which he meant the nave] is well pewed with *English Oak*, and regular till of late years, that some Seats are advanced at the West End and more remote parts, for Persons of Distinction not before provided for; those for the Mayor, Aldermen and the Vicar, are raised at the East End, and under the North Wall [presumably on the far side of the most northerly aisle] for the Master and Mistress of the Charity School together with forty poor boys and girls 'decently clad in blue'.[31] In 1720 'two Convenient Galleries' were erected for the Charity Children on either side of the organ, and it was decided that 'the seats of the north side of the church [presumably where the Charity Children had formerly sat] be altered so as to face the pulpit'.[32] There was a balustrade (or staircase up to) one of the charity school children's galleries (Fig. 1.8).

Two additions to the nave were completed just in time to be included in Thoresby's addendum. The gallery on the south side of the nave was added in 1715, and an organ was financed by subscription in June 1713, and completed at a cost of about £250 in 1714. He described it as 'a very fine large Organ; the Case whereof is adorned with a very curious carved Work; the Front Pipes laid over with right Gold, the Whole containing near thirteen hundred Speaking Pipes, was performed by Mr. Hen. Price Organ-builder.' It was topped by the carved figure of St Peter, which today adorns the porch of the Minster.[33]

Moving on to the crossing, Thoresby continued: 'At the Meeting of the great middle Isle with the large cross Isle, the Steeple is founded upon 4 prodigiously large Pillars and Arches'; these were concealed in

Fig. 1.7: 'View of the Nave looking East, with the Altar in the Distance, showing Font, Pews, Galleries, Pulpit, Organ', c.1838 by Joseph or John Rhodes. (By kind permission of Leeds Libraries, www.leodis.net)

Fig. 1.8: 'View of the South Transept from the North' *c*.1838 by Joseph or John Rhodes. (By kind permission of Leeds Libraries, www.leodis.net)

Fig. 1.8: 'View of the South Transept from the North' *c*.1838 by Joseph or John Rhodes. (By kind permission of Leeds Libraries, www.leodis.net)

Rhodes' view, as they were in Thoresby's time, by the organ.[34] 'Against one of these Pillars stood the Pulpit in the Days of Yore, when there were no Seats in the Nave of the Church; for before the Reformation there were no Pews or different Apartments allowed, but the whole Body of the Church was common, and the Assembly promiscuous or intermix'd, "in the more becoming postures" of Kneeling or Standing.'

The north transept

Walking under the tower arches and looking left, the visitor saw the north transept; Thoresby referred to this as the 'Queen's Isle'. In the Rhodes view of it (Fig. 1.9), we see the large Gothic north window and a second font with a beautiful, richly crocketed spiral cover. The apparent brightness and airiness of this transept is striking and no doubt was due to the improvements overseen by William Cookson in the 1710s. Thoresby noted in his addendum that: 'The Windows before darkened with fragments of painted Glass (of which not one Figure remained whole) are now entirely new glazed with large Squares, (fortified with Iron in place of the more cumbersome Wood Stanchions.' Major Moore writing in 1877 remembered the font, but was unsure what had become of it.[35] Its fate is still unknown, but the monuments on the walls were preserved and placed in the Victorian church.

The wooden screen on the right gave entry to the north aisle of the chancel and the former Lady Chapel. Above the screen is the King's Arms, which greatly intrigued Ralph Thoresby: 'The King's Arms is curiously perform'd in Basse-Relieve, supported by the Lion and Unicorn, whose Statues are very artificially contrived to appear right, both in the Quire and Body of the Church.' Fortunately, the Arms were retained and can still be seen in the identical position in the Minster.

The south transept

Turning on their heels and looking past the font and the back of the organ, visitors would have seen the south transept, where Thoresby identified the Chapel of St Katherine as having been. The transept as seen in the Rhodes painting (Fig. 1.8) was much altered from Thoresby's day because part of the south wall of the church had been rebuilt and a more 'correct' window inserted by the local architect Thomas Taylor between 1808 and 1812.[36] A notable feature of the new window was the stained glass, of which there was very little in the church in Thoresby's day. At its centre is the image of St Peter which in 1837 was attributed to Mr Smith 'an ingenious artist of the town'.[37] Happily, today the stained-glass St Peter is incorporated in the present-day St Peter's window on the south side of the nave of the Minster, reminding us that the church's dedication is to St Peter.

The quire or chancel

Progressing through the tower crossing arches, Thoresby takes us into the 'Quire' or chancel (Figs 1.10 and 1.11) which he was anxious to point out was exceptional in character: 'What is most surprising to

Fig. 1.9: 'View of the North Transept Northwards, Showing Font and Cover, with Royal Arms on Right' c.1838 by John Rhodes. (By kind permission of Leeds Libraries, www.leodis.net)

strangers is the spaciousness of the Quire or Chancel, which is within the Walls as much above 88 foot one way, as it wants of 60 the other. … This is monthly fill'd (for the most part) twice round with devout communicants, one of the most blessed prospects this world affords, besides much greater numbers upon publick festivals.'[38] The downside of this was that over two-fifths of the church was very little used in the Georgian period; worship principally took place in the nave which effectively was a preaching box.

Nevertheless, in the early eighteenth century considerable sums had been expended on the redecoration, enhancement and provision of additional pews in the chancel. In the Rhodes' view of the High Altar (Fig. 1.10) its enhanced glory is revealed (though as other views make clear, for much of the week in the 1830s it was concealed by huge green curtains to keep it from dust and light). In the main part of *Ducatus*, Thoresby notes: 'Behind the Communion-Table, which stands upon an Ascent (of three Steps) that takes up the entire Breadth of the high Quire is placed a new Altar-piece of right Wainscot; the Intercolumn is Scarlet Cloth adorn'd with Gold Fringe, &c. with these Words of the Apostle *Christ our Passover is sacrificed for us* writ in Letters of Gold. The whole surrounded with Rails and Banisters.' Though wary of any imputation that Leeds would have any truck with Popery, he adds 'But these Ornaments are only for Decency or Conveniency'. Nevertheless, in his addendum, with enormous pride he enthuses: 'Monsieur James Parmentier, a celebrated artist, desirous to express his Gratitude for the

Fig. 1.10: 'View of the Altar', *c.*1838 by Joseph or John Rhodes. (By kind permission of Leeds Libraries, www.leodis.net)

Encouragement he had here met with in his employment, bestowed upon the Church a most noble specimen of this Art, viz. the *Giving of the Law*, the Thunder and Lightning at the rending of the thick clouds, are expressed (in fresco upon the Roof) in suitable Terror, but qualified by the lovely Aspects of a Choir of Angels and Cherubs, with *Moses and Aaron* in the clouds, &c. The Decalogue, Creed and our Lord's Prayer, are well performed (with the Painter-stainer's Work) in Letters of Gold upon Tablets of black Marble, by John Seynor of this Town.'

In the Rhodes painting we see the black marble tablets with the Ten Commandments, the Creed and the Lord's Prayer, with Moses and Aaron surrounded by the choir of angels and cherubs. The painting of the Last Supper between the altar wainscot and the *Giving of the Law*, was painted and installed in 1717, again by Parmentier. At the same time the communion rail was enlarged and the wainscot of the high altar 'was made uniform with the painting'; the latter appears to have been an entirely new structure composed along similar but more elaborate architectural lines.[39] Sadly, this altar piece did not survive the rebuilding of the church, but Parmentier had already painted an almost identical rendering of *The Last Supper* in oil for the high altar of the medieval parish church of Holy Trinity, Kingston-upon-Hull in 1711–12; this has survived in that church, though in a poor and truncated state.[40]

Thoresby was also excited by other recent improvements including the provision of an elaborate 'candlestick'. These can be seen in Figure 1.11, the Rhodes painting showing the chancel looking west from the

Fig. 1.11: 'Westward View of the Chancel from the Altar', *c.*1838 by Joseph or John Rhodes. (By kind permission of Leeds Libraries, www.leodis.net)

altar platform to the organ which emphasises the considerable width produced by the aisles. Thoresby continued: 'The high Quire [is] new ceiled, to which the Right Honourable Juliana, Countess Dowager of Burlington, gave twenty pounds, in gratitude to which the Impropriators Arms with the Quarterings (for the noble Families of Clifford, Seymor, and Noel) and Supporters very well painted, are now [in] placed. … Even while I am writing this, another Ornament is added, viz. a noble Brass Candle-stick, with thirty Branches, the Accoutrements painted and gilt, said to equal the best in the North of England. The Skreen and Seats in the Quire, the Pillars there, and through the Nave of the Church, with the Galleries, are all new painted in a decent manner.'

Two of the Rhodes paintings (Figs 1.12 and 1.13) respectively look across three aisles of the chancel to its north-east corner with the altar on the right, and from the organ gallery to the north-east corner of the chancel once occupied by the Lady Chapel. These views, in addition to Figures 1.10 and 1.11, highlight the almost complete absence of stained glass from the chancel in the 1830s, the removal of which, as we have seen, seems to have dated from Thoresby's time. The views also show pews lining all the walls of the chancel; their date is uncertain.

Thoresby rejoiced in this addendum at the overall impact of the recent improvements: 'The Parish Church, which was said before (p. 39) to be an Emblem of the Church Militant, black but comely, does now flourish as a Bride adorned with her Jewels, and though the Altars might be more pompous in the Times of Popery, we may safely conclude that

Fig. 1.12: 'View of the Altar from the South Aisle of the Chancel' c.1838 by Joseph or John Rhodes. (By kind permission of Leeds Libraries, www.leodis.net)

Fig. 1.13: 'View looking over the Organ Screen to the North-East corner of the Chancel', c.1838 by Joseph or John Rhodes. (By kind permission of Leeds Libraries, www.leodis.net)

the entire Church was never so beautiful since its Foundation.' Reining himself in, lest his readers might think he had any Roman Catholic sympathies or love of religious ornament, he declared: 'The chief glory of this church is, that upon the Lord's-day it is generally filled with a vastly great and attentive congregation, which is the most comfortable sight a pious Christian can behold.'

Alterations to the church 1740–1837

Between 1726 and 1740, little work seems to have been done to the fabric of the church, while the prosperity of the town around it grew significantly with the growth of trade, manufacture, and freight on the Aire and Calder Navigation. By this time Leeds was enhancing its position as the seventh largest town in England. Over the next century there were few alterations to the church. The Bucks' *Prospect of the Town of Leeds* published in 1745 conveys the character and prosperity at this time of this wealthy centre of the woollen cloth industry (Fig. 1.14). The tower of the Parish Church can be seen in the centre of the image; the tower and spire to its right is that of Holy Trinity Church, Boar Lane, the fashionable church erected in the 1720s primarily to accommodate the wealthy merchant and professional classes; virtually all its pews were sold or rented to private individuals.

In the early 1740s a new frame was erected in the tower to house eight bells. In 1743 the completion of 'the Chimes in our Parish Church' was reported: 'they play four Times upon eight Bells in a very elegant

Fig. 1.14: Parish Church shown on *The South-East Prospect of Leeds, in the County of York* (1745) by Samuel and Nathaniel Buck.

Manner.'[41] In 1772–3 a new vestry room designed by John Carr was added to the east end of the church.[42] In 1778 a new gallery was built at the west end of the nave, and the north and south clerestory window of the nave were enlarged primarily to admit more light to the side galleries. At the same time, two 'Sky Lights' were recommended for the south aisle and a further three were installed over the north aisle.[43] These incredibly ugly, boxy skylights can be seen on the north side of the church (Fig. 1.6), and the interior of one of them can be glimpsed above the gallery in the south aisle of the nave (Fig. 1.7). On 3 July 1778 attention focused on altering 'the large Gothic Window at the West End', with two sections each in the lower and upper frames 'made to open'. At the end of 1778, the rebuilding of the north gallery was under consideration and tenders were received, but we cannot be sure that the work was carried out.[44] Describing the character of the nave and some of its potential structural weakness on the eve of its demolition, Major Moore noted that: 'Long, projecting, and unsightly galleries were suspended from the west end and from the north and south walls. The clustered columns of the fourteenth century were nearly cut through, as also the pointed arches to accommodate the same. The approaches or stairs to each gallery were dark and cumbrous; and, for light, the roofs were pierced, and huge, ugly dormer windows erected therein.'[45]

The Parish Church in the nineteenth century

The Revd Thomas Dunham Whitaker included a fine engraving of the church from the south-west in his monumental book, *Loidis and Elmete* published in 1816 (Fig. 1.15). Though the engraving makes the church look very impressive and cathedral-like, in his text Whitaker was frank about its deficiencies: 'The parish church of Leeds has few pretensions to elegance, but it has a solid substantial air of unpretending dignity, not ill suited to an opulent commercial town.' Recalling Thoresby's comment that the church in his day was 'black but comely', Whitaker observed that 'Unhappily, since [Thoresby's] time it has become more black, but certainly not more comely.' He noted that the great East window has been 'dispensed with … it is now obstructed partly by the altar screen and partly by the erection of a very large and commodious vestry' (see Fig. 1.5). Philosophically, he opined that 'On the deformity of the galleries which incumber this church, it would be worse than idle to complain. We ought rather to be thankful that they are wanted. In a place of worship, elegance and uniformity, however desirable when

Fig. 1.15: Parish Church from the south-west. (By Thomas Taylor, published 1 May 1816, in T. D. Whitaker, *Loidis and Elmete* (Leeds, 1816))

they can be attained, are very inferior considerations.' Anticipating improvements which Hook was later to seek, he made some practical suggestions: 'A very material improvement might be effected, at little expense of room, by removing the organ to the west end, and opening the whole perspective of the church from thence to the altar. St. Peter, whose statue now surmounts the organ, would then regard the altar of his own church, and be visible from thence.'[46]

Some fine monuments were added to the church in the first four decades of the nineteenth century, particularly those commemorating sons of the wealthy Leeds middle classes killed in the wars of those years. Most notably are the monuments to Col Thomas Lloyd, commander of the Leeds Volunteer Infantry, and to Captains Samuel Walker and Richard Beckett who were killed at the Battle of Talavera in 1809.

The stripping out of the church

Dr Hook's arrival as vicar in 1837 was to seal the fate of the medieval church, as Christopher Webster will explain in the next paper. We are unusually fortunate that the Rhodes chose to paint three views of the interior of the church when it was being stripped out in preparation for its demolition. These views allow us to see clearly the structure of the medieval church unencumbered by the organ, pews and galleries, and give an impression of the bustle as the workmen went about their jobs. In Figure 1.16 the east window can be seen for the first time, and the west window in Figures 1.17 and 1.18. The large piles of dismantled pews and

Fig. 1.16: View looking south-east from the nave with view of east window, interior fittings and monuments being removed, 1838 by Joseph or John Rhodes. (By kind permission of Leeds Libraries, www.leodis.net)

Fig. 1.17: View looking west through the crossing arches to the west window, interior fittings and monuments being removed, 1838 by Joseph or John Rhodes.
(By kind permission of Leeds Libraries, www.leodis.net)

wainscot, scattered carelessly about the floor of the church, make us fear for the wanton destruction of historic fixtures and monuments.

It is not clear what happened to Monsieur Parmentier's altar paintings but, as Margaret Pullan's study of the monuments and memorials in the present-day Minster shows, there was an earnest effort to conserve the wall monuments and gravestones from the medieval church wherever possible.[47] Indeed, because the new Parish Church occupied the same footprint as its predecessor, the wall tablets and monuments were able to be redisplayed in positions close to their equivalent locations in the old church, and seemingly few monuments and memorial tablets were lost.

In the process of demolition, there were discoveries great and small. The finding of the Anglo-Danish crosses was the most dramatic one, though the recognition of their huge importance was insufficient to prevent the architect Chantrell from removing them to his home. On a much more minor scale, Major Moore later recalled: 'In taking down the galleries and pews, the lumbersome staircases, casings, wainscoting, etc,

Fig. 1.18: View looking north-west from the chancel, interior fittings and monuments being removed, 1838 by Joseph or John Rhodes. (By kind permission of Leeds Libraries, www.leodis.net)

under the flooring were found a great number of fans of various sizes, shapes and periods, smelling bottles, vinaigrettes, coins, toothpicks, knives, gloves, book markers, brooches, pins, etc., etc., and an immense accumulation of the *dust of ages*.'[48] Also he noted that: 'At a considerable depth under the chancel floor and within the communion rails was also found with its face downwards a mutilated stone effigy of a cross-legged knight. On removing the old vestry and taking up the floor, it was found to be laid upon skulls, thigh and arm bones, to the depth of two feet, ostensibly for the purpose of keeping it *dry*.' The effigy of the knight can still be seen in the Minster today. In contrast, contemporary newspaper reports suggest that no great effort seems to have been made to retain in their existing locations the buried bodies and coffins disturbed by the rebuilding work.[49]

The merits of the replacement of the medieval Parish Church by its Victorian successor will be discussed in subsequent papers; but, for those who seriously regret its loss, the retention of the memorial tablets, gravestones and artefacts of the former church must at least provide some consolation.

Notes

1. S. Burt and K. Grady, *A History of Kirkgate from Earliest Times to 1800* (Leeds, 2016), pp. 1–2. For the general context, see S. Burt and K. Grady, *The Illustrated History of Leeds* (2nd edition, Derby, 2002).

2. The Venerable Bede, *Historia Ecclesiastica* (1896), pp. 115–116. For discussion of this point see L. Butler, 'Medieval Leeds' in A. Mason, ed., *Religion in Leeds* (Stroud, 1994), 13–14; also P. Ryder, *Medieval Churches of West Yorkshire* (West Yorkshire, 1993), 15–24. The location of the Roman fort of Campodunum has never been identified.

3. A. McGuire and A. Clark, *The Leeds Crosses* (Leeds, 1987).

4. Butler, 'Medieval Leeds', pp. 14–16; Ryder, *Medieval Churches*, pp. 10–14.

5. G. R. Jones, 'To the Building of Kirkstall Abbey', in M. W. Beresford and G. R. Jones (eds.), *Leeds and its Region* (Leeds, 1967).

6. J. Le Patourel, 'The Norman Conquest of Yorkshire', *Northern History*, VI (Leeds, 1971), 1–21; W. E. Wightman, 'The Yorkshire Lacys, 1066–1193', *University of Leeds Review*, X (Leeds, 1966).

7. Information about the relations between Holy Trinity Priory and Leeds Parish Church comes from Revd J. Solloway, *The Alien Benedictines of York* (Leeds, 1910).

8. E. K. Clark, 'A Brawl in Kirkgate', *Thoresby Society Publications* [PTS], IV (1895), pp. 125–138. Also described in Burt and Grady, *Kirkgate*, p. 12.

9. I am grateful to Dr Paul Barnwell for this insight into the significance of the central tower. He notes that central towers ceased to be built in new churches because the large arches required on all four sides of the base of the towers created dead space between the nave and the chancel and reduced the visibility of the altar. Moreover, from the thirteenth century major structural weaknesses often occurred when the number of bells increased (some heavier than before) and with the beginning of swinging the bells.

10. Solloway, *Alien Benedictines*, pp. 70–71.

11. Major R. W. Moore, *A History of The Parish Church of Leeds* (Leeds, 1877), p. 2. Moore in his preface commented: 'It appears to have devolved upon myself as pupil of the architect, (with whom I was during the whole time of pulling down the old and erection of the present edifice, and having had my share in making the working drawings, &c, and also of superintending the execution thereof,) to give an account of the same, and hand it down to future generations.'

12. T. Fenteman, *An Historical Guide to Leeds and its Environs* (Leeds, 1858), p. 51.

13. R. Thoresby, *Ducatus Leodiensis* (1715), second edition, ed. T. D. Whitaker (Leeds 1816), p. 39.

14. Burt and Grady, *Kirkgate*, p. 10.

15. J. Rusby, *St Peter's at Leeds being an Account Historical and Descriptive of the Parish Church*, J. G. Simpson, ed. (Leeds, 1896), p. 22.

16. Moore, *History*, p. 7.

17. Transcript in M. W. Beresford, 'Leeds in 1628: A "Ridinge Observation" from the City of London', *Northern History*, X (1975).

18. Burt and Grady, *Illustrated History*, pp. 40–42.

19. Moore, *History*, p. 8.

20. Thoresby, *Ducatus*, pp. 26, 40. In her will of 1545 Julia Jeffaryson, the mother of Sir Thomas Jeffrayson, chantry priest at the altar of St Mary Magdalen in the Parish Church, asked to be buried 'nye the trinitie quere, where as my father and mother was buried'. 'Testamenta Leodiensis', PTS, XIX (Leeds, 1913) p. 125. The Rockley Quire was founded by the Rockley family whose house was in the Lower Head Row. In his will of 1506 William Dyneley ordered his body to be interred on the south side of the Rockley Quire nigh unto his wife; T. D. Whitaker in his *Loidis and Elmete* (Leeds, 1816), p. 50, with some reluctance followed the suggestion of the antiquary Thomas Wilson that the chapel was on the south side of 'the high choir, a clue to its location being the family's coat of arms in stone being to be seen 'on the east end, on the outside'.

21. I am particularly grateful to Dr Roy Yates for his advice regarding the medieval church's chantry chapels.

22. Ralph Thoresby, *Vicaria*, p. 22, mistakenly located the chantry on Briggate – at 'the corner-house on the West side of the great street'.

23. Whitaker, *Loidis and Elmete*, p. 71.

24. 'The Certificates of the Commissioners Appointed to Survey the Chantries, Guilds, Hospitals, etc., in the County of York', *Publications of the Surtees Society*, XCII (1893), pp. xiv, 215.

25. Rusby, *History*, p. 26. The priests were Reginald Parke, William Townend, Henry Smyth, John Eure (probably the brother of the vicar), Thomas Cartell, Thomas Heryson, and John Brayton.

26. Rusby, *History*, pp. 27–32.

27. R. V. Taylor, *Biographia Leodiensis: Worthies of Leeds* (Leeds, 1865), pp. 395–96; W. H. Thorpe, *John N. Rhodes: a Yorkshire Painter, 1809–1842* (Leeds, 1904).

28. Terry Friedman's detailed account of the physical changes to the church and its furnishings during the eighteenth century can be found on pp. 10–42 of his masterful study: T. Friedman, 'Church Architecture in Leeds, 1700–1799', PTS, second series, vol. 7 (Leeds, 1996).

29. Thoresby's description of the church is in *Ducatus*, pp. 39–60, 247–48.

30. This font, shown in Figure 1.7, at the west end of the church had been installed in 1662. Today it stands in the Minster near the south-west door but is no longer used. It was superseded in 1883 by an elaborate marble font designed by William Butterfield.

31. Thoresby, *Ducatus*, p. 40. Friedman, *Church Architecture*, p. 15 mistakenly suggests that the new pews referred to were in the chancel.

32. Cited in Friedman, *Church Architecture*, p. 33.

33. Friedman, *Church Architecture*, pp. 18–19; Thoresby, *Ducatus*, p. 248.

34. Whitaker footnote in Thoresby, *Ducatus* p. 40: 'The South Gallery was erected in February 1713. The gallery on the north side of the west end was erected in 1778.' He added that the black cloth was 'exchanged in 1785 for Crimson Velvet for the pulpit and purple for the desk'. The candlestick was put up 27 October 1711. The organ was put up in Aug. 1714 for which the subscription amounted to £500. 12s. 6d. The Ascension was painted by Vanderbank in 1748.'

35. Moore, *History*, p. 27. This second font looks medieval in style, and most probably had been superseded by the font in the nave; though Major Moore said that 'it was supposed that the font which stood in the North Transept was the one ordered to be made and placed in the church, Feb. 3rd, 1662'.

36. E. Parsons, *The Civil, Ecclesiastical, Literary, Commercial and Miscellaneous History of Leeds* (Leeds, 1834), vol. 2, p. 420.

37. William White, *History, Gazetteer and Directory of the West Riding of Yorkshire*, vol. 1 (Leeds, 1837), p. 514.

38. Thoresby, *Ducatus*, p. 40.

39. R. Thoresby, *Vicaria Leodiensis* (1724), Preface; Friedman, Church Architecture, p. 32.

40. Friedman, *Church Architecture*, pp. 24–31.

41. Friedman, *Church Architecture*, p. 33.

42. Friedman, *Church Architecture*, p. 36.

43. Friedman, *Church Architecture*, p. 37.

44. Friedman, *Church Architecture*, pp. 40–4.

45. Moore, *History*, p. 4.

46. Whitaker *Loidis and Elmete*, p. 51.

47. M. Pullan, The Monuments of the Parish Church of St Peter-at Leeds, *Thoresby Society Publications*, second series, vol 17 (2007).

48. Moore, *History*, p. 8.

49. *The Leeds Times*, 1 May 1841.

2.
Dr Hook's New Parish Church (1837–41)

CHRISTOPHER WEBSTER

As noted in the Preface, on 2 September 1841, the day of the consecration, the eyes of the Anglican world really were on Leeds. The huge number of clergy who travelled from across the country to attend the service – perhaps as many as 400[1] – testifies that this was not just 'another' new church at a time when they were being erected across England at a rate of around 100 per year (see Fig. 3.4);[2] Leeds Parish Church was certainly special. It was the largest new church erected in England since St Paul's in London and 'as grand as any cathedral'.[3] The *Church of England Magazine* concluded 'The church is one of the noblest in the kingdom'.[4] However, its significance came not just from its size and magnificence. To understand its importance, we need, briefly, to examine wider issues associated with the Church of England at this time.

Throughout the late-Georgian period, the Church of England occupied a decidedly precarious position. While it was, indeed, the Established Church, it was conscious of the threat from the rapid growth of Nonconformity and, to a lesser extent, from Roman Catholicism. In addition, there was the worrying spread of atheism. Nonconformity was widely seen as having a more direct appeal to the working families, especially in the expanding industrial towns.[5] Indeed, when Hook arrived in Leeds, he noted 'the *de facto* established religion here is Methodism'.[6]

Across the country, there was a desperate shortage of church accommodation; many that wanted to worship in their local church were unable to find a seat as post-Reformation church-building had conspicuously failed to keep in step with a rising population. The problem was most prevalent in rapidly increasing manufacturing communities like Leeds and it was one most keenly felt by the poor who invariably struggled to find a seat in their local church. While this problem was widely acknowledged, initiatives to build in order to counter it were often hampered by the cumbersome legal framework in which the Church of England was compelled to operate. Being the Established Church offered certain protections, but this also dictated Parliamentary oversight which hampered local initiatives.[7] These laws, many dating back centuries and initially put in place for perfectly legitimate reasons, were, by the nineteenth century, hopelessly outdated and left the Church ill-equipped to adapt to changing circumstances, as noted in Christopher Hammond's paper. Meanwhile, the Nonconformists and Roman Catholics were free to build wherever they wished with almost no legal obstacles.

Consequently, many friends of the Church, although deeply worried about the situation, felt totally ill-equipped to confront the problem. However, Hook was widely seen as a man of vision and energy – 'the greatest parish priest of the nineteenth century', according to James Rusby – and one determined to act while others merely lamented the challenges. Thus in Leeds, in 1841, came together all the crucial ingredients in the longed-for *national* Anglican revival: a magnificent new building, a charismatic and energetic cleric, and a parish ripe for regeneration. Hook's ambitious plans to reinvigorate the huge parish were keenly followed by the entire Anglican community. It is not an exaggeration to claim that Hook played a very significant part in laying the foundations of Anglican worship for the modern age, a theme to which we will return in this paper. His Leeds Parish Church remains exceedingly impressive and, remarkably, has had few alterations since 1841.

This paper has four themes: the evolution of the architectural design; the internal planning and Hook's radical liturgical arrangements; the use of new materials and processes in Chantrell's design, especially internally; the critical reception of the newly completed building.

1. The evolution of the design

Kevin Grady has already discussed the medieval church which preceded the present one. When Dr Hook was appointed to the Leeds living on 15 April 1837, apparently he complained that the church was 'nasty, dirty, ugly [and] old'.[8] More specifically, it was one in which it was impossible for him to conduct the services with appropriate decency, a crucial issue for Hook, one which is addressed later in this paper and in the one by Kenneth Powell. The old, medieval church might have worked reasonably well for pre-Reformation worship, although this is questionable; the problem was always that the central tower, with its closely spaced pillars, essentially cut the church in two (see Fig. 1.5).

Certainly it presented real problems for the post-Reformation period as, through the seventeenth and eighteenth centuries, Anglican liturgy developed into what is now referred to as 'auditory worship', or as the Victorians dismissively called it, 'preaching box worship'. Auditory worship involved the congregation listening and reflecting, and thus, in principle, learning. It implied a passive role for worshippers but one where their ability to hear was paramount. It was quite different from sacramental worship widely promoted later in Victoria's reign in which there was greater emphasis on ritual, ceremonial and associated visual effect. Crucially, much Victorian opposition to Georgian worship and ecclesiastical architecture was underpinned by their endeavours to push worship in a Higher – that is, a more sacramental – direction.

In the auditory tradition, the regular services – Morning and Evening Prayers – were led by a cleric at a three-decker pulpit, strategically placed in the church to be as close to the worshippers as possible and thus maximise their ability to hear (Fig. 2.1).[9] To satisfy this mode of worship in Leeds, the principal worship space had developed in the nave of the old church (see Fig. 1.7). Here an almost self-contained auditory church had been created. There were galleries around all four sides, and seats focused on the pulpit, some facing west with their backs to the altar. Meanwhile, the east half of the church – the chancel – was almost cut off from the nave and used only for the occasional Communion service (see Fig. 1.10). These are themes to which we will return.

Fig. 2.1: The Philanthropic Society Chapel, London, view looking west (James Peacock, 1803–6) as it appeared around 1810. (Engraving after a drawing Auguste Pugin & Thomas Rowlandson from *The Microcosm of London*, London, 1808–10)

This was, unquestionably, an inefficient arrangement as less than half the available space was used for the principal weekly services. By 1837, there was a desperate need for more accommodation in the town and Hook quickly realised that the church could be used more efficiently.[10] Indeed, his own popularity exacerbated the problem with increasing numbers of congregants having to stand through the service and late-comers being turned away.

Within days of his arrival, he was considering changes to the building. Although the project eventually developed into a four-year long almost total rebuilding, Hook's initial ideas were modest, as announced in the *Intelligencer* on 29 April 1837. This proposal was essentially to provide more space for ground floor seats and to raise part of the roof so that more galleries could be erected, all within the existing outer walls. The estimated cost was £2–2,500.[11] Perhaps at this stage, the ideas were entirely Hook's. However, by July 1837 we know Hook was in discussion with 'an [un-named] architect', almost certainly this was R. D. Chantrell, an eminent Leeds designer and the most experienced ecclesiastical architect in the county. Subsequently, the Bishop of Ripon described him as 'one of the [leading] architects in the north of England'.[12]

By early October 1837 the *Leeds Intelligencer* reported discussions which included moving the tower from the crossing to the north transept. While, ideally, the tower needed to be re-sited to open up the interior, placing it at the west end would have been more conventional. However, by placing it over the north transept, the tower gained real prominence when seen from the centre of the town, a prominence it would not have had in a conventional western location. The estimated cost was now £4,500.[13]

On 19 October, Hook had a meeting with some of the leading townsmen and it was agreed that Chantrell should be formally appointed for the job. Chantrell apparently accepted willingly and two days later, the *Intelligencer* reported that a plan 'to raise the whole roof [and make] new internal arrangements' had been accepted. The estimated cost was now £6,000.[14]

Many in the town were immediately enthused. Also in October, Hook received an address from at least 600 parishioners requesting him to call a meeting to discuss enlarging the church; this took place on 8 November. However, Hook didn't want just more seats, he also wanted a more dignified setting for his services where the liturgy and ritual of the Church of England 'might be performed with solemnity and grandeur', something impossible in the old church.[15] Equally importantly, Hook wanted a church which would generate the appropriate messages, an impressive Gothic design that was not only a confident statement of Anglican ambition, but was also redolent with notions of tradition, a potent reminder of a distant, but meaningful, Anglican heritage looking back to the true and undivided Church.[16] Indeed, he believed 'a handsome church is a kind of standing sermon'.[17] It was an arena in which the Nonconformists struggled to compete.

At the November meeting, Hook announced a plan to add 1,200 extra seats, 700 of which would be free.[18] He was given enthusiastic support and Chantrell's proposals were formally accepted. Chantrell immediately began working on detailed plans and later that month, the faculty, necessary to authorise the work, was applied for. This was accompanied by four plans, drawn by Chantrell, showing the existing arrangement and the proposed changes (Figs 1.5, 2.2, 2.3, 2.4).[19] Figure 1.5 reveals the narrowness of the tower arches that supported the tower and the absence of seating in the chancel, while the plan of the proposed new ground floor arrangement shows the tower removed from the crossing to the north transept (Fig. 2.2). Also revealed is that the nave, crossing and chancel were to be widened. All the internal columns were to be new and most were to be re-sited. They would rise to support new clerestories and the clerestories would, in turn, support

Fig. 2.2: Leeds Parish Church, proposed ground floor plan. Chantrell's initial design for the faculty for renovation, 1837. (Borthwick Institute, York, Faculty 1837/5)

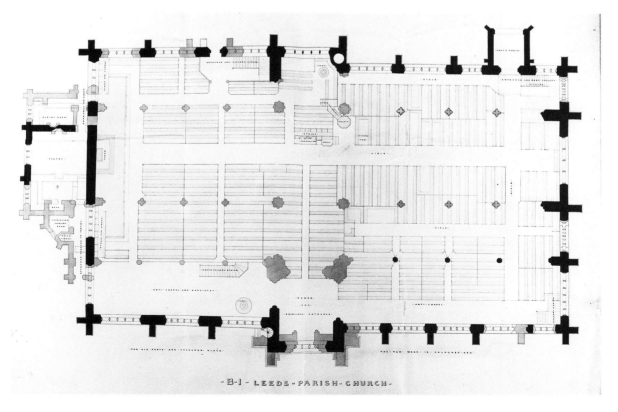

-B-1- LEEDS-PARISH-CHURCH-new, higher roofs. Very significantly, at this stage *all* the outer walls were to be retained, changed only by the introduction of a small number of new windows, and new tracery in most of the old windows. Note the organ that had seriously divided the church in two was to be moved to the north gallery (Figs 2.3, 2.4). The whole church could now be used as a single entity. It was to be pewed throughout, and with substantial galleries around three sides continuing to the east wall and enclosing the altar which, in this proposal, had only a modest space around it to allow for maximum seating.

While the 1837 plans make clear Hook's desire for the maximum number of seats, some more progressive ideas are certainly present in this initial scheme. Significantly, the altar was given prominence and was intended to be within sight of almost all the huge congregation. Furthermore, there was to be no three-decker pulpit, something near ubiquitous in churches at this time. Rather, the 1837 plans reveals a self-contained pulpit and a separate reading desk, attached to a desk for the clerk. Remarkably, there are ground-floor 'STALLS FOR CHORISTERS', situated in the crossing, opposite the organist in the north gallery (Fig. 2.2).

The *Intelligencer* of 17 February 1838 invited builders to tender 'for renovating the eastern part of the church'. However, the following week,

Fig. 2.3: Leeds Parish Church, gallery floor plan as existing in 1837. (Borthwick Institute, York, Faculty 1837/5)

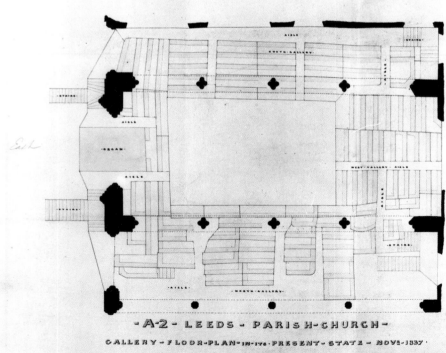

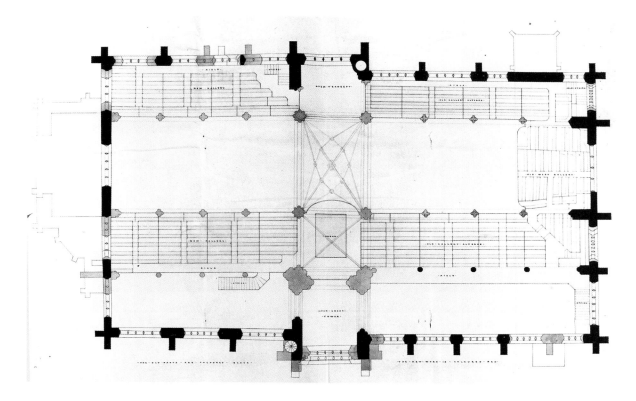

Fig. 2.4: Leeds Parish Church, proposed gallery floor plan. Chantrell's initial design, 1837. (Borthwick Institute, York, Faculty 1837/5)

the paper published a letter from 'an old inhabitant' suggesting that this was an ideal opportunity to build an entirely new church. The same edition quoted 'a member of the Building Committee' as saying this was quite out of the question.

The church closed in March 1838 and rebuilding work started. Only as plaster and wooden casings were stripped out did the full extent of decayed stonework and poor foundations become evident. Despite the emphatic rejection of the 'old inhabitant's' call for a new church, just two weeks later another letter appeared in the *Intelligencer*. This one was signed 'Dionysius' – almost certainly Chantrell using the Latin form of his middle name – stating that 'the south wall alone is to be retained, the remainder being razed to the foundations'. The same edition of the newspaper invited builders to tender for renovating the whole building.[20]

The following month – April 1838 – Chantrell prepared a further set of drawings (Figs 2.5, 2.6). These were to accompany a grant application to the Incorporated Church Building Society.[21] These reveal some significant changes from the plans from six months earlier that accompanied the faculty and, importantly, in these 1838 plans, almost all the key elements of the scheme that was completed in 1841 had been

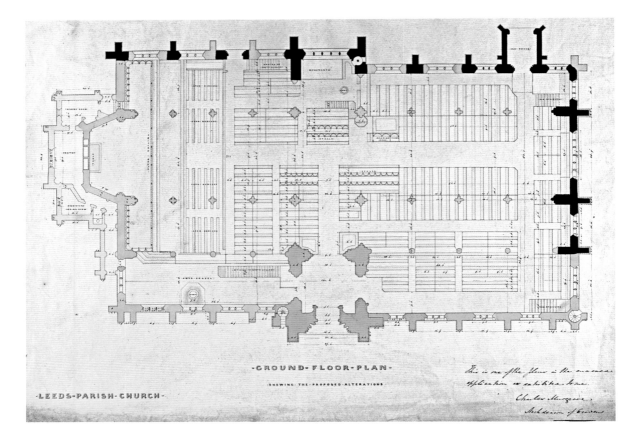

·GROUND·FLOOR·PLAN·

SHEWING THE PROPOSED ALTERATIONS

·LEEDS·PARISH·CHURCH·

Fig. 2.5: Leeds Parish Church, ground floor plan. Chantrell's second design of April 1838. (ICBS, file 02293, Lambeth Palace Library)

settled upon. Consequently, while the internal arrangements of the finished church, consecrated in 1841, were certainly radical, three years earlier, in 1838, these proposals were significantly more radical.

A comparison between Figures 2.2 and 2.5 is revealing. The entire east and west walls were now to be new; the altar is in an apse with more space around it. This 'new' east end is similar to that at St Michael, Coventry, a church which Hook would have known well from his time in the city. Moreover, the drawings reveal a remarkable seven steps up to the altar, a staggeringly radical idea for 1838 and certainly one that invited Hook's opponents to claim he had popish sympathies. Also important is that the eastern bay of the chancel is now without any pews at either ground or gallery floor level to provide more dignity to the altar. And there is now more accommodation in the crossing for the choir.

Construction progressed. By November 1839, the estimated cost had risen to £19,000[22] and by the time of completion almost £30,000 had been spent.[23] To put this in context, at almost the same time that the church was being rebuilt, Chantrell built a substantial new church

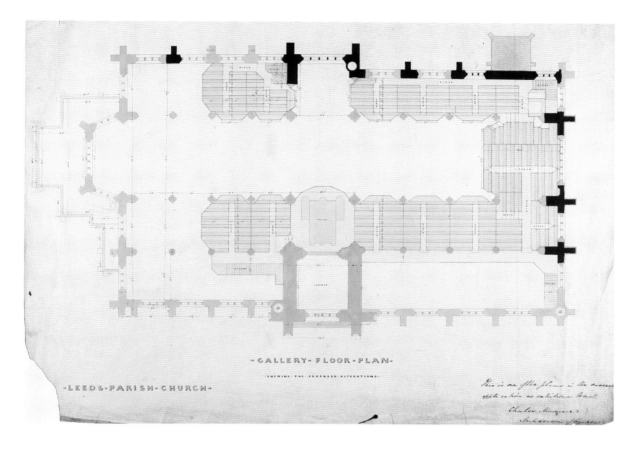

-GALLERY-FLOOR-PLAN-

-LEEDS-PARISH-CHURCH-

Fig. 2.6: Leeds Parish Church, gallery floor plan. Chantrell's second design of April 1838. (ICBS, file 02293, Lambeth Palace Library)

in Skipton. It cost £6,260 while the rebuilding of the little chapel at Pool, near Otley, initially had a budget of just £308.[24] One senses that from 1839, around the mid-point of the project, Hook enjoyed such support in the town that money was no object. The leading citizens of Leeds just kept giving.

Between 1838 and 1841, there were further modifications to the design (compare Figures 2.5 and 2.7). In the final plan, the south transept was extended outwards by twelve feet to accommodate the organ, now removed from the north gallery.[25] And there is a discrete reading desk and significant space around the font. There is accommodation for an even larger choir and both this and stalls for the clergy have moved from the crossing to the chancel. The decision to place the choir stalls there and include stone 'altar rails' came in August 1840.[26] Although Figure 2.7 shows 'additional seating' on the altar flat and central aisle, it is not clear that the altar flat was ever actually used for seating, although extra seating in the central aisle certainly existed well into the twentieth century. A plausible explanation for the extra seating appearing in this drawing is that it 'confirmed' to the ICBS that its grant had provided a huge amount

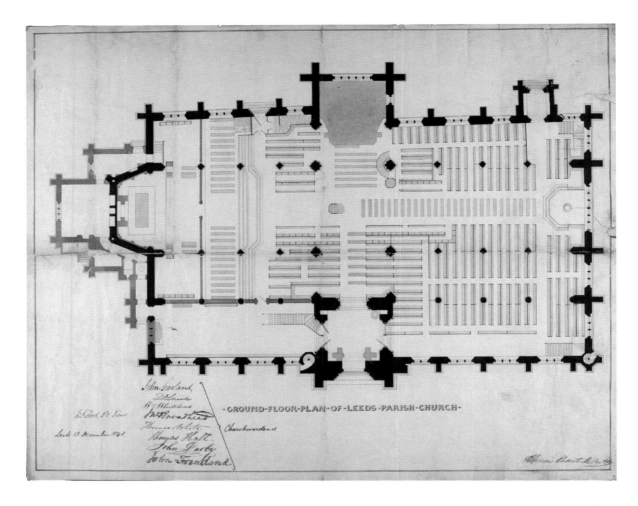

·GROUND·FLOOR·PLAN·OF·LEEDS·PARISH·CHURCH·

Fig. 2.7: Leeds Parish Church, ground floor plan, December 1841, Chantrell's final design. (ICBS, file 02293, Lambeth Palace Library)

of additional accommodation. In the finished church, the ground floor was given over to free seats and there are no seats on the altar flat.

Also interesting is the decoration of the internal walls of the clerestory, something that is not in the 1838 drawings, but appeared in the finished church. This moulded decoration, rising slightly above the bottom of the windows, is an unorthodox arrangement and is likely to have been inspired by a similar feature in the Cathedral in Bruges, Belgium, which Chantrell was currently restoring following a fire (see Fig. 2.21).

Hook later explained the rebuilding process. 'Bit by bit, we found the church crumbling about us, and were placed in the predicament of building a new church, not repairing an old one'.[27] The crucial, but unanswered question is this; had Hook and Chantrell known from the start that almost nothing of the old church would survive and that an awesome £30,000 would be spent, would a very different church have been designed? The answer is likely to have been 'yes'. Yet despite rising costs and lengthening project times, there was widespread enthusiasm in the town for its new church, even in the pro-Nonconformist *Leeds Mercury*. So far as the pro-Tory *Intelligencer* was concerned, the recipients of its praise were threefold: Hook for his vision, Chantrell for the way he overcame the endless constructional problems, and the subscribers to the project. At the consecration, the *Intelligencer* noted that the new church 'is truly an honour to Leeds and those who have contributed to the work ought to consider it one of the privileges of their lives'.[28] The newspaper also recorded, 'In nothing was the genius of the architect more strikingly displayed than in the skill with which Mr Chantrell availed himself of the circumstances as they occurred. What would have perplexed an architect of fewer resources was only, for him, an opportunity to evince his power'.[29]

The exterior

In Hook's drive to reassert the Church of England in Leeds, image was of crucial important, both for those worshipping within it, as well as for those merely walking past. With the limited means at his disposal, Chantrell responded commendably. For the commanding exterior, he chose a phase of Gothic which he described as a

> transition from the Decorated to the Perpendicular style, which has its peculiarities, though unnoticed by modern writers on Gothic architecture, and admits of a variety of form which the others do not; the masses partake, more generally of the Decorated character, but the flowing arch of the minuter parts terminate gracefully in the vertical tracery of the windows, and where no tracery is above it, finials form the termination of the cusped arches of the transoms; after this the whole forms become Perpendicular and in the fifteenth century was nearly abandoned.[30]

This eloquent statement clearly showed Chantrell's research and came, let us not forget, at a time when, according to *The Ecclesiologist*, 'church architecture … [was] generally ill understood'![31] The richly panelled tower is especially impressive, and the asymmetry it represented was an early example of this in England, and certainly well ahead of the Ecclesiologists' advocacy of it (Fig. 2.8).[32] Throughout the design, Chantrell's scholarship is apparent. For several of his earlier ecclesiastical commissions he was explicit about his studies of medieval examples in Yorkshire and these are well recorded;[33] for his final Leeds Parish Church design, elements of York Minster's west towers can be identified

Fig. 2.8: Leeds Minster from the north. (Roy Tuangco)

in the Leeds tower and the two octagonal turrets on the north elevation suggest Chantrell had looked carefully at those at St Mary, Beverley; the north-west one at Leeds containing a spiral staircase and bell was added to the design in 1841. The elaborate parapet decoration on the tower and east end comprising rows of slender pinnacles above delicate arches reflect similar features on the tower of All Saints, Pavement, York. Other external details confirm his research using the available illustrated books, especially those by Britton and the Pugins, father and son.[34]

2. Liturgical planning

One of the most significant aspects of the new church was its internal arrangement, carefully planned to enable Hook's radical liturgical ideas to be fully displayed; in these, it is reasonable to assume that Chantrell was guided by the vicar. While the interior might, in the twenty-first century, appear unremarkable, that is precisely because the church set the pattern for so much that became almost universally accepted in the worldwide Anglican community. But in 1841, this really was ground-breaking. This is a point that can best be made by putting Leeds Minster in context.

An examination of some typical pre-1840 examples is revealing, for instance, the Philanthropic Institute Chapel, London, opened in 1806 (Fig. 2.1) or St John, Islington, London, from 1828 (Fig. 2.9). In both, the importance of the three-decker pulpit is unambiguous; it occupies the most prominent location and is the focus of the congregation. However, in both examples, the huge pulpits obscure sight of the altar, widely seen as regrettable, but a reasonable sacrifice to provide the congregation with the most efficient acoustic. An alternative arrangement survives at Old St Stephen, Fylingdales, North Yorkshire, with a pulpit on the south side of the nave and with some seats having their backs to the altar (Fig. 2.10). Although apparently novel, it was far from unique, popularised by its capacity to bring the majority of the congregation close to the pulpit. Indeed, it had much in common with the contemporary arrangement in Leeds. Many other examples could be quoted. It is easy to forget what the interiors of pre-1840 churches looked like because they were so comprehensively changed by the Victorians in the second half of the century, but these examples were entirely typical. And they provide context for the Rhodes view of the inside of the old Parish Church which Hook inherited (see Fig. 1.7).

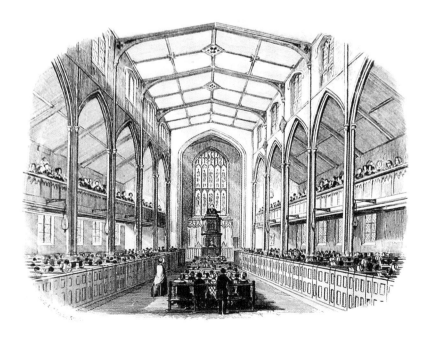

Fig. 2.9: St John, Islington, London (Charles Barry, 1828). This shows an entirely typical arrangement for a new church in which a packed congregation, focused on the huge pulpit, listen intently. (Engraving, c.1830)

Fig. 2.10: 'Old' St Stephen, Fylingdales, North Yorkshire (1821–2). The pulpit is placed in the centre of the south wall, with the cleric's script well lit from behind. Although not obvious in this photograph, downstairs pews west of the pulpit face east, while those east of the pulpit face west. (Geoff Brandwood)

Fig. 2.10: 'Old' St Stephen, Fylingdales, North Yorkshire (1821–2). The pulpit is placed in the centre of the south wall, with the cleric's script well lit from behind. Although not obvious in this photograph, downstairs pews west of the pulpit face east, while those east of the pulpit face west. (Geoff Brandwood)

These seating arrangements worked remarkably well for late-Georgian auditory worship; these interiors were, as William Whyte deftly commented, 'machine[s] for listening in'.[35] However, Hook was determined to have something more sacramental. While it is clear he rejected Anglo-Catholicism, he was certainly intent on making his services more dignified and introducing certain Higher practices to his services, and in this respect, he really was a pioneer.

Hook was determined that the magnificent altar would be the focus in all services and would be clearly seen by almost all the congregation (Fig. 2.11). Thus it was raised on seven steps for maximum prominence and the pulpit was placed on the south side of the central aisle where it would not obstruct this view. The huge crossing arches that Chantrell designed facilitated this in a way that a conventional – narrower – chancel arch would not have done. And one of the most important innovations in Hook's church was the placing of the choir stalls between congregation and altar – absolutely the norm through the second half of the nineteenth century, but almost unheard of beyond the cathedrals in 1841. Indeed, the plan was 'epoch making'.[36]

Standing in the crossing today, looking east, one sees so much that soon became the norm for Victorian worship of a Higher type: a huge chancel, steps up to the altar, and choir stalls for a robed choir. It also has a vast altar flat where worshippers could gather when invited to 'draw near with faith' before taking Communion.[37]

Although the Ecclesiologists were influential in many ways, initially the group had no real use for the substantial chancels they demanded on the grounds of medieval precedent, beyond a place for the altar and stalls for the clergy. In 1841, they were still urging church-builders to put choirs in west galleries.[38] Not until 1843 did the Ecclesiologists promote the idea of choirs in chancels, a full two years after the opening of Leeds Parish Church.[39] As Owen Chadwick crisply noted, Hook gave the Ecclesiologists a 'use for their chancels'.[40] In arranging the choir stalls in the chancel, Hook received advice and encouragement from John Jebb, and his uncle, also a John Jebb, Bishop of Limerick, both of whom he knew while still in Coventry and before coming to Leeds.[41]

Having a robed choir placed between altar and worshippers in a parish church was a significant innovation. 'The first church of any note in which it was adopted is the present parish church of Leeds', claimed Addlershaw and Etchells.[42] In this respect, Hook and the Jebbs were not looking to the cathedral tradition in which the chancel was largely cut off from the congregation in the nave, but to the traditions of the basilican churches of the fourth or fifth centuries.[43] Both Hook and the Jebbs believed it was essential for the congregation to be able to see the altar, something often not possible when seated in a cathedral nave where there was a substantial choir screen.

Hook believed that the choral service was 'one of the finest expressions of faith.' And certainly a good choir could make a profound musical contribution to services, a point noted by several

Fig. 2.11: Leeds Parish Church, view looking east. Note the civic pews, left and right foreground with the choir stalls further east. Also significant is the richly decorated altar and reredos and the seven steps up to it. (Engraving after a drawing by W. Richardson, detail of frontispiece)

commentators. A robed choir also made a memorable visual statement: at the start of the service no longer did a lone cleric walk through his crowded congregation to reach his pulpit; now he could be preceded by a uniformed verger leading a substantial choir. It really was a liturgical revolution. As noted in the Preface, George Washington Doane, bishop of New Jersey, made the 3,000 mile journey across the Atlantic to preach at the consecration and learn more of Hook's liturgical innovations, seeking to introduce them in North America. And aspects of the Leeds internal arrangement – especially the congregational seating and location of the choir – reached Australia and could be found in St Andrew, Sydney, and Christ Church, St Lawrence, both completed in the mid-1840s and both the work of the architect Thomas Blacket, a man with Yorkshire connections, who emigrated to Australia in 1843.[44]

3. Seating the congregation

Among the significant features of the church is its seating. Although at first glance it appears unremarkable, in several respects it is a very rare survival of once common features; in others it is near unique.

We have already considered Hook's ambition for the maximum number of seats, but the final design was far from cramped. This was another example of Hook's desire for 'dignity'.

The civic pews

Through the Georgian period, most substantial towns designated one of its churches as the civic church. It was here that the civic dignitaries worshipped: the mayor, alderman, judges and magistrates. These churches generally received financial support from the civic purse; in the case of Liverpool, the council even built its own church, St Luke, erected regardless of cost. Elsewhere, the town council might contribute to repairs to the church, or pay the salary of an eminent organist. Or it might pay for a professional choir.

There is one very remarkable aspect of Georgian and early-Victorian civic church-going. While religious ceremonial had almost completely disappeared from services, civic ceremonial became increasingly grand, almost theatrical in some towns. Every Sunday, at the civic church, would be seen a procession of the dignitaries in their civic robes, led by the mace-bearer and various beadles. And the entourage would be handsomely accommodated in designated civic pews.

This blending of religious and secular authority was an anathema to many Victorians and the ritual disappeared. Almost all civic pews also disappeared. For instance, the civic churches of Nottingham and Manchester became cathedrals and were reordered; Doncaster's burnt

Fig. 2.12: Leeds Parish Church, the Mayor's pew.

down and Liverpool's was bombed. Thus the civic pews in Leeds are a very rare survival (Figs 2.11, 2.12). Here, the best of the civic pews are, remarkably, misericords and are grandly decorated (Fig. 2.13). The mayor's pew bears the town coat of arms.

Other seating

Seating for the rest of the congregation is equally engaging with examples that are of interest both for their design and their construction. Some are now exceedingly rare. When the church opened in 1841, the galleries contained entirely rented pews, while downstairs, with the exception of the civic pews, were the free seats (Fig. 2.14). This is not the place to explore the ethics of pew renting, but whatever thoughts of elitism might be generated for a twenty-first century audience, pew renting was an absolutely essential aspect of the financial well-being of almost all churches at this time and was widely used in Nonconformist chapels too. As elsewhere, each rented pew was carefully valued by the churchwardens: the closer to the pulpit the gallery pew was, the more rent it commanded. The principle was that a pew closer to the pulpit made it easier for the occupants to hear the sermon and – at least as importantly – such a pew also gave prominence to its occupants.

The north-east and south-east galleries are engaging survivals, real time-capsules of early-Victorian church-going: many are cramped and with very poor views of both the pulpit and altar, but they retain their numbered doors and some still have their 'private' lockable boxes intended to contain the tenant's bibles and prayer books (Fig. 2.15).

Fig. 2.13: Leeds Parish Church, one of magistrates' misericord pews.

Fig. 2.14: Leeds Parish Church, view looking west. (Lithograph by Shaw and Groom, published c.1841)

Fig. 2.15: Leeds Parish Church, the south-east gallery.

Fig. 2.16: Leeds Parish Church, a fold-down seat. The seat marked with the red paper can be raised to allow for entrance and exit. Once the family is in the pew, the flap can be lowered to create the extra seat and once the door is closed, it becomes the back of the seat.

Fold-down seats

Fold-down seats were an ingenious way to create an extra seat in a pew. There are several examples of this once-common feature in the church (Fig. 2.16). Part of the seat can be raised to allow for entrance and exit. Once the family is in the pew, the flap can be lowered to create the extra seat and once the door is closed, it becomes the back of the seat.

Fig. 2.17: Leeds Parish Church, a pew end of one of the rows of free seating on the ground floor. The Gothic decoration is of cast iron, comprised of six identical members, screwed to the plain wooden framework. The vertical decorative members are of wood as is the outer boarder including the curved corners.

Fig. 2.18: The clergy stall on the south side of the chancel. The upper line of pointed arches use the same iron castings as those in Fig. 2.17.

Materials

The seating in Leeds Parish Church is also a rare survival of the latest material and technological developments. For instance, much of the decoration on the pew ends and the fronts of the principal pews is of cast iron, screwed onto plain wooden panels and used as a cheaper substitute for carved wood (Figs 2.17, 2.18). Some of the screw holes are easily spotted (Fig. 2.19). And the galleries are supported by slender cast-iron columns. In 1841, galleries were absolutely the norm in new churches, but even at this date, Chantrell – in complete harmony with the Ecclesiologists – confessed that they 'were at all times defects. Thus they are supported by small iron pillars; placed behind, and independent of, the stone pillars which support the clerestory and roof, to denote that they, like the pews, are mere furniture.'[45] However, he acknowledged their necessity to provide adequate accommodation. Such columns were once common, but disappeared, along with the galleries they supported as the Victorians condemned them for lacking medieval precedent.

The most conspicuous material innovation is the papier mâché decoration on the gallery fronts, which passes convincingly as carved wood (Fig. 2.20). Papier mâché was not a new material, but it gained considerable prominence following the 1834 publication of C. F. Bielefield's book on the subject.[46] Its use here was dictated by the need for economy. It is well known that, later in the nineteenth century, the Victorians, and especially those advocating Arts and Crafts principles, were obsessed with 'real' craftsmanship and the 'honest' use of materials. Papier mâché clearly failed on both counts. But through the first part of the nineteenth century, new materials were celebrated. Not only were

Fig. 2.19: Detail of Fig. 2.18 revealing the screw heads.

Fig. 2.20: Part of the north-east gallery showing the elaborate Gothic pinnacles of papier mâché on iron armatures.

they economical, but they were symbols of Enlightenment thinking and Britain's world-leading technological advances, and were thus proudly developed. And if, during the construction of this church, a generous donor had approached Dr Hook with an offer of a huge sum of money so that real carved pinnacles could have been placed on the gallery front, it is very likely that he would have replied that this donation could have been used far more productively in the building of a new school, or a small church. To spend more than was necessary on the gallery fronts Hook would have seen as a flagrant misuse of precious resources.

4. The critical reception of the new church

In his 1842 publication, G. A. Poole, an antiquarian-minded, Tractarian cleric and prolific author, gave a list of those recent churches that gave 'encouragement and hope' to those seeking better ecclesiastical architecture. He included 1830s examples by Thomas Rickman and H. J. Underwood – two of the most accomplished ecclesiastical architects of the age –adding 'but noblest among the noble [is] the Parish Church of Leeds.'[47]

The nationally-circulating journal, the *Church Intelligencer*, reviewed the building a week after its consecration. It gives a sound indication of contemporary attitudes: 'We trust we shall have no more churches in the bald and beggarly style of dissenting meeting houses, unworthy of God and disagreeable to those who build them, but in the manner of the magnificent church at Leeds which stands as a noble monument to the taste, the sterling Christianity, and the old-fashioned

Fig. 2.21: View looking east, taken from the west gallery, 2010. (Blacksheep photography)

piety and spirit of Churchmanship of that town.'[48] John Jebb thought the 'arrangements in every respect Catholic',[49] an opinion with which *The Ecclesiologist* concurred: 'It is the first great instance of the Catholic feeling in a church, energising rudimentally – thrown off, by a strong, vigorous mental effort, the mere preaching house, grasping at the altar as being, rather than the pulpit, the central point of worship … '[50] (Fig. 2.21).

Poole predicted the 'stately interior' would have 'no limited or transient effect on the ecclesiastical architecture of this kingdom.'[51] He was quite correct: the eastern half of this largely unaltered 1841 interior really does predict so much that would soon become the norm in world-wide Anglican worship.

Notes

1. John Mayhall, *The Annals of Yorkshire*, 2 vols (Leeds, 1862), 1, 472; Anon., *The Seven Sermons Preached at the Consecration …* (Leeds, 1841), lxv-lxxvii, lists 300 named clergy, but stated that 'there were many clergymen present whose names were unknown'.

2. A.D. Gilbert, *Religion and Society in Industrial England* (London and New York, 1976), 28, states 2,194 new churches were built between 1831 and 1851.

3. Owen Chadwick, *The Victorian Church*, 2 vols (London, 1971), 1, 413.

4. *Church of England Magazine*, 11, 1841, 'Register of Ecclesiastical Intelligence', October 1841, 28.

5. Among many sources that could be quoted, see Mark Smith, *Religion in Industrial Society, Oldham and Saddleworth 1740–1865* (Oxford, 1994); J. A. Hargreaves, 'The Georgian and early Victorian church in the parish of Halifax, 1740–1851' in *Transactions of the Halifax Antiquarian Society*, 1991.

6. W. R.W. Stephens, *Dean Hook*, 2 vols (London, 1879) 1, 243.

7. See Christopher Webster, 'Late-Georgian Church-Building: the Legal and Administrative Challenges' in *Ecclesiology Today*, 61, 2022, forthcoming.

8. Stephens, *Hook*, 1, 401.

9. Interestingly, and as a counter to claims that the Parish Church was entirely moribund before Hook's arrival, in addition to Sunday services, there were three 'prayer' services every week day. Edward Baines, *History, Directory and Gazetteer of the County of York* (Leeds, 1822), I, 24.

10. Twenty years earlier, Whitaker had suggested removing the organ and its gallery to open up the church and views of the altar. T. D. Whitaker, *Loidis and Elmete*, (Leeds, 1816), 51.

11. *Leeds Intelligencer*, 29 April 1837.

12. Lambeth Palace Library, Church Building Commission papers, file 26725.

13. *Leeds Intelligencer*, 7 October 1837.

14. *Leeds Intelligencer*, 21 Oct 1837.

15. *Leeds Intelligencer*, 11 Nov 1837.

16. H.W. Dalton, 'Walter Farquhar Hook Vicar of Leeds' (PTS, Leeds, 1990), 40.

17. *Leeds Intelligencer*, 11 November 1837; Stephens, Hook, 1, 382.

18. *Leeds Intelligencer*, 11 Nov 1837.

19. Borthwick Institute, York, Faculty Papers, 1837/5.

20. Leeds Intelligencer, 10 March 1838.

21. Lambeth Palace Library, ICBS papers, file 02293.

22. Leeds Intelligencer, 30 November 1839.

23. Mayhall gives the cost at £29,770. 6s. 8d. Mayhall, *Annals*, 1, 472.

24. See Christopher Webster, *R. D. Chantrell (1793–1872) and the architecture of a lost generation* (Reading, 2010), 303–5; 300.

25. This was decided in January 1839, LPC archives, 41/8, WYAS.

26. LPC archives, 41/7, WYAS.

27. *Leeds Intelligencer*, 30 November 1839.

28. *Leeds Intelligencer*, 4 September 1841.

29. *Leeds Intelligencer*, 23 October 1841.

30. *Leeds Intelligencer*, 29 August 1841.

31. *The Ecclesiologist*, 6, n.s. 3, 1846, 116.

32. *The Ecclesiologist*, 1, 1842, 53.

33. Lambeth Palace Library, CBC Minute Book 26, p. 234; Minute Book 32, 300–1.

34. LPC archives, 41/7, WYAS.

35. William Whyte, *Unlocking the Church* (Oxford, 2017), 43.

36. G.W.O. Addleshaw and Frederick Etchells, *The Architectural Setting of Anglican Worship* (London, 1948), 211.

37. It was a tradition inherited from the old church. See R.W. Moore, *A History of the Parish Church of Leeds* (Leeds, 1877), 4–5; E. Kitson Clark, *A History and Description of St Peter's Church at Leeds* (London n.d.), 7.

38. Addleshaw and Etchells, *Architectural Setting*, 209; Cambridge Camden Society, *A Few Words to Church Builders* (Cambridge, 1841), 23.

39. *The Ecclesiologist*, 3, 1843, 1–5.

40. Chadwick, *Victorian Church*, 1, 413–4. Hook received advice about church music and where to place the choir from John Jebb. See Jebb, *Choral Service*, 152.

41. Addleshaw and Etchells, *Architectural Setting*, 210.

42. Addleshaw and Etchells, *Architectural Setting*, 213.

43. Addleshaw and Etchells, *Architectural Setting*, 214.

44. Derek Linstrum, *West Yorkshire Architects and Architecture* (London, 1978), 217.

45. *Leeds Intelligencer*, 4 September 1841.

46. C. F. Bielefield, *Ornaments, Drawn from Examples Executed from the Improved Papier Mâché*, (London, 1834).

47. G. A. Poole, *The Appropriate Character of Church Architecture* (London and Leeds, 1843), 12.

48. *Church Intelligencer*, 11 September 1841.

49. Jebb, *Choral Service*, 209.

50. *The Ecclesiologist*, 8, N. S. 5, 1848, 132.

51. Poole, *Appropriate Character*, iv.

3.

'There's High Church, Low Church and there's Leeds Parish Church': the Liturgical Tradition

KENNETH POWELL

'Internally, probably the country's most important church of its date': the verdict of *The Buildings of England* on the parish church of St Peter, Leeds.[1] The church was constructed in 1837–41, replacing, and largely following the footprint of, a large, cruciform medieval church which, a decade or so later, would probably have been retained and restored. The construction of the new church, at a cost of nearly £30,000, was

Fig. 3.1: Revd Dr Walter Farquhar Hook, oil painting by William Beetham, 1842, now displayed in the church.

the work of the architect R. D. Chantrell, a pupil of Sir John Soane who had practised in Leeds for two decades. His client was Walter Farquhar Hook (1798–1875), vicar of Leeds from 1837 to 1859 (Fig. 3.1).

Hook came to Leeds at a time when the town was growing exponentially as a major industrial and commercial centre – its population more than doubled in thirty years. The Church of England had responded to the challenge of a rapidly growing population with a series of new churches built in the 1820s using funds supplied by Parliament via the Church Building Commission. (The most ambitious, Christ Church, Meadow Lane, was the work of Chantrell.) But Hook was sceptical of the impact of the new churches which had the status of chapels of ease to the parish church, and which, according to Hook's biographer (and son in law) W. R.W. Stephens, were 'total failures'. They were without endowment, the congregations were very scanty, and the stipend derived from pew rents was next to nothing'.[2] The parish church remained the centre of Church life in Leeds, the venue for the great majority of baptisms, marriages and funerals, but was otherwise moribund. 'The Vicar on his arrival found the surplices in rags and the service books in tatters, but the churchwardens doggedly refused to spend a farthing upon such things. When they assembled at the church for a vestry meeting, they and others like-minded piled their hats and coats upon the holy table, and sometimes even sat upon it; but the new Vicar with stern resolution quickly put a stop to such profane outrages.'[3] Hook quickly concluded that the church building, as it stood, was an obstacle to his vision of the liturgy. He wrote to a friend: 'such a church as I have! I really loathe it; I cannot preach comfortably in it, I can scarcely make myself heard; and the dirt, the indecorum, etc, etc, quite distress me ... I seek to exhibit to the world the Church in her beauty; let the services of the Church be properly performed, and right-minded people will soon come to love her.'[3] As it stood, the services in the church, when they took place, had been 'most slovenly performed'. Writing to the Revd T. H. Tragett in August, 1837, Hook wrote of the 'dirty, ugly hole of a church in which it is impossible to perform divine service properly; the chancel for example, being formed into an almost distinct church, and the body of the church being arranged to look as near as possible like a conventicle' (see Figs 1.9, 1.6).[4] In the same letter he announced his intention for a partial rebuilding of the church, to cost no more than £4,000. Stephens, writing after Hook's death, conceded that 'there can be little or no doubt that in the present day some parts of the old structure, and the general character of the whole, would have been preserved; and the extreme dislike of the Vicar to the church ... arose from his inability to detect the real beauties which were concealed beneath deformities of modern growth.'[5]

Hook's churchmanship was rooted in the Laudian tradition. He stood apart from the Oxford Movement, launched by John Keble's Assize Sermon on 'National Apostasy' in July, 1833. 'I love Pusey, Newman and Keble with all my heart and soul', he wrote, 'but I call no man Master'.[6] Nonetheless his vision of the Church of England – 'an idiosyncratic mixture of traditional and Tractarian principles' – was in tune with that of the Oxford Movement.[7] Fundamental to that vision was Hook's commitment to the Eucharist as the central act of Christian worship, rather than Morning and Evening Prayers which, across the country, had become the standard weekly services. Indeed, in 1843 the sacrament of the Lord's Supper was administered 77 times.[8] 'The Church teaches us that in the blessed Eucharist the body and blood of Christ are verily and indeed taken by the faithful'.[9]

Hook's campaign to revive the Parish Church as the central pivot in the revival and renewal of Church life in Leeds has been celebrated as an outstanding success. Beyond the Parish Church, his achievements as a church builder were heroic. Under the terms of the Leeds Vicarage Act (1844) the parish of St Peter, Leeds, was divided and the 20 chapels of ease became parish churches. Hook declared that 'unless the Church of England can be made in the manufacturing districts the church of the poor, which she certainly is not now, her days are numbered'.[10] This theme is discussed in more detail in Christopher Hammond's paper, Paper 5.[11]

The parish church of St Peter remained the central focus of Hook's work. It had seen a period of revival during the incumbency of John Killingbeck (1690–1715). Killingbeck had established a monthly celebration of Holy Communion and was a frequent and eloquent preacher. Hook's immediate predecessor as vicar (1815–37) was Richard Fawcett – he 'belonged to the past and, as the years of his incumbency wore on, it became increasingly evident that, if the church were not to fall hopelessly out of the progress of the nineteenth century a man must be found whose sympathies were large enough to grasp the future. The Vicar of Leeds must be something more than a scholar and a gentleman.'[12] Fawcett died suddenly in January, 1837, leaving a sad legacy: 'the Vicar of Leeds and his two curates had given up the struggle, or rather, had never realised it. They went on preaching, baptizing, marrying and burying, while the very conception of the Church had faded from the minds of their parishioners.'[13] Clearly, Victorian commentators had every reason to exaggerate the achievements of a new generation of dynamic, reforming clergy and to dismiss those of a preceding generation but Hook's impact on church life in Leeds was indisputably dramatic.

Richard Fawcett established a professional surpliced choir in the parish church as early as 1815, placed in the east gallery, next to the organ.

Up to 1827, it was maintained by a charge on the church rate, and paid, very reluctantly, by those parishioners who did not worship in the church, especially the Nonconformists. It was disbanded at some point between 1833 and Hook's arrival.[14] Surpliced choirs, seated in stalls in chancels, became a feature of most Anglican churches by the end of the nineteenth century;[15] Hook was a pioneer of this development. A key influence on his thinking was John Jebb (1805–86), nephew of John Jebb, Bishop of Limerick from 1823 to 1833 and resident, as an invalid, at Leamington Spa in the last years of his life, where Hook became friendly with him and got to know his nephew. Jebb junior, prebendary of Hereford, the author of Three Lectures on the Cathedral Service (1841), delivered in Leeds in the same year. 'Cathedral Service', fully choral, as prescribed by Jebb, became standard practice in Leeds, in contrast to the more congregational style of worship in other High churches, such as All Saints, Margaret Street. Jebb commented: 'at Leeds, every part of the Liturgy, on the evenings of all weekdays, and at all the services on Sundays and Holidays, is performed according to the strictest and best Choral precedent, those parts even being sung which are usually omitted in Cathedrals.'[16] Jebb argued that 'in the constitution of her choirs the Church of England has made the nearest possible approach to a primitive and heavenly pattern. Her white-robed companies of men and boys, stationed at each side of her chancels, midway between the porch and the altar, stand daily administering the service of prayer and thanksgiving.'[17]

Hook's radical transformation of the liturgy was powered by the force of his personality. Soon after his arrival in Leeds, the *Leeds Mercury*, 'the organ of the dissenters', commented: 'his style of reading the prayers and liturgy is admirable. There is a solemnity and energy in the manner which give a powerfully increased effect to the simplicity and beauty of the forms. Indeed, it was a universal remark at the conclusion of the service that he is incomparably the best reader that ever occupied the pulpit in the parish church'.[18] Hook was clearly an impressive preacher. His first sermon in the parish church on 16 April, 1837, made a powerful impression: 'his rich, powerful, melodious voice produced its full effect upon the musical ears of the northern people, and he had not proceeded far in the prayers before a godly old Dissenter present was heard to say, smiting his knee with his hand, 'He'll do; he'll do'.[19] But the central focus of Hook's work in Leeds was the establishment of a liturgical routine in which the Eucharist had a central part. Hook established a pattern of worship in which Holy Communion was celebrated at least once every week. (In the later years of his ministry an evening celebration was introduced but, in line with

Tractarian teaching, was swiftly discontinued by his successor, James Atlay.) On weekdays, Morning Prayer was said daily and Evensong sung at 7.30 p.m. In Lent, four services took place every day at 7.30 a.m., 11.00 a.m., 3.00 p.m. and 7.30 p.m., with Hook preaching every evening. All Sunday services were sung to choral settings. In 1842 Samuel Sebastian Wesley – the most celebrated church musician of his day – was recruited to direct the newly established choir, remaining in Leeds until his move to Winchester Cathedral in 1849.

The new parish church was designed to accommodate the large – surpliced – choir of men and boys that was the foundation of the new liturgical regime established by Hook. (In 1851 a service commemorating the 10th anniversary of the building was sung by a choir of no fewer than 90 voices.)[20] Chantrell's church was designed to accommodate a large choir, with an impressively elevated position for the altar in an eastern apse, as demanded by Hook (Fig. 3.2). Between the choir stalls

Fig. 3.2: The interior, looking east, lithograph by Richardson, 1841 (detail), showing the original altar and altar surround. The mayor's pew is in the bottom left and further east, left and right, are the choir stalls. Just behind the choristers is the eagle lectern.

and the sanctuary, a generous space was provided where communicants could 'draw near' at the Invitation in the service of Holy Communion, an arrangement that was not taken up in subsequent church building projects. This substantial altar flat can be linked to an older tradition in the church going back perhaps to the seventeenth century. In the old church, the chancel 'was spacious enough for three or four hundred persons' to move forward to the altar at the Invitation.'[21]

The altar was covered by a velvet carpet given by the dowager Queen Adelaide, with a painting of the Agony in the Garden ('after Correggio')

Fig. 3.3: A view east from the crossing showing the altar flat in front of the communion 'rail' and the uninterrupted view of the altar. (Geoff Brandwood)

Fig. 3.4: Leeds Parish Church from the north-east on the day of the consecration, showing robed clerics and other dignitaries approaching the church. Lithograph by Richardson and Hawkins, 1841.

as reredos and there were two candlesticks. This was not quite the earliest revival of altar candles – Littlemore had them in 1837 and Margaret Chapel, London, in 1839 – but it was certainly a pioneering example and a clear statement of Hook's churchmanship (Fig. 3.3). (The sanctuary was completely refitted in the 1870s and 80s, with a reredos by G. E. Street now the dominant feature.)

Hook made the consecration of the new church a memorable occasion that epitomised the style of his ministry in Leeds. 'Such a concourse of prelates, clergy and laity had probably never been seen in any provincial town in England in modern times … The church was thronged with thousands of all ranks; upwards of one thousand communicated, and the offertory amounted to £620–14–0d'. (Fig. 3.4).[22] The preacher was George Washington Doane, Bishop of New Jersey, hymnologist, publisher of the American edition of Keble's *Christian Year*, and 'as complete a specimen of a High Church Bishop as this world has seen'.[23] A youthful Florence Nightingale, who was in the congregation, noted 'it was quite a gathering for Puseyites from all parts of England'.[24]

Hook's liturgical ideas certainly impressed, and sometimes astounded, worshippers. Indeed, in September 1842, Hook told Pusey that no cathedral in England could match the services at Leeds Parish Church for solemnity and grandeur'.[25] The Bishop of Tasmania, visiting Leeds that year, recorded that 'he had never seen anything to equal the sublime effect of the liturgy of the Church of England as performed in the parish church of Leeds, heightened by the attention, the devotion and the decorum of the crowded congregation.'[26] The following year, a

Fig. 3.5: St Saviour's, Leeds, looking east. (Philip Wright)

visitor noted: 'The service was conducted according to the strict letter of the rubric, and with a fervor and solemnity of manner, which gave it a proud pre-eminence over those similar establishments where the pure and beautiful language and formularies of the Protestant church are sacrificed to the rapid and careless manner of the officiating priest … The prayer for the church militant, the absolution, the consecration of the sacrament elements, and the administration of the Holy Sacrament, were said and performed with becoming solemnity … We had never previously seen or heard the services of the English Church so impressively conducted, and we left that house of God fully impressed with the conviction that the influence of the example here set would rapidly effect wondrous changes in the manners, habits and religious opinions of British society, from which manifold blessings, spiritual and temporal, will inevitably follow.'[27]

However, and despite Hook's desire for dignified services and his obvious High Church sympathies, his support for the Tractarian movement – he pronounced himself 'with them but not of them' – was severely strained by the events following the opening of St Saviour's church, located a mile from the parish church and funded by Pusey (Figs 3.5 and 3.6). The defection to Rome, in 1847, of five members of the clerical community that had been established at St Saviour's was a bitter blow. Hook wrote: 'I was beginning to feel that Leeds had become to me a perfect Paradise, and now it is a howling wilderness … I have fought for the Church of England against the Puritans, so will I now fight for her against the Romanisers.'[28] Hook's attitude to the subsequent rise of Anglo-Catholicism can only be surmised, but the relatively moderate character of the movement in Leeds perhaps owes something to him. (Hook's son Cecil moved from Chichester in 1874 to become the vicar of All Souls, Leeds, the Hook Memorial Church and a major Anglo-Catholic centre.)

By around 1850, liturgical change became widespread across the country. This radical development gradually came about from the mid-1830s as the Oxford Movement encouraged greater piety and placed more emphasis on the sacraments and on the apostolic tradition. All of this nudged Church of England worship in a Higher direction. And in late 1839, the Cambridge Camden Society was formed – a group later known as the Ecclesiologists – and literally built on the initiatives emanating from Oxford. Together, they successfully rehabilitated Higher worship for early-Victorian Anglicans. But, very significantly, it was not until the mid-1840s that new churches of the type promoted by either the Oxford Movement or the Ecclesiologists began to appear. Leeds Parish Church, of 1841, really was a pioneer.

The liturgical tradition established by Hook persisted into the 20th century. By the 1870s there were two celebrations of the Eucharist on Sundays and Holy Days. By the 1890s, during the incumbency of E. S. Talbot, the Eucharist was celebrated daily with a formal Sunday Sung Eucharist established in the 1920s, with the eastward position, mixed chalice and lighted candles.[29] One of Talbot's curates recalled: 'we had the surplice and the black stole and nothing more. We had two lights upon the altar, and we took the eastward position'.[30] Talbot's successor, E. C. S. Gibson, later Bishop of Gloucester and a member of the Royal Commission on Ecclesiastical Discipline, had to answer charges brought by a militant Protestant in 1904 regarding the manner in which the Eucharist was celebrated.[31] By the 1900s the ceremonial at the parish church was a common feature of many 'moderate' parishes. Leeds Parish Church did not move forward in liturgical matters. It was not until the 1980s that Choral Mattins was supplanted by the Sung Eucharist as the principal Sunday service. (A monthly Choral Mattins continued until 2013.) Eucharistic vestments were not in regular use before the incumbency of Canon Jim Richardson in the 1980s. Richardson's predecessor, Graham Foley, celebrated wearing a cope, though Fr Stephen Jones, Precentor 1976–79, had begun to assemble a collection of vestments. Reservation of the Blessed Sacrament, in an aumbry in the Lady Chapel, began in the 1990s.[32]

In 1986 Gavin Stamp wrote of Leeds Parish Church – where Evensong was still being sung daily – that it 'represents that element

Fig. 3.6: A satirical drawing, by one of the Leeds Parish Church curates, shows Hook, caught between the Evangelical and Nonconformist press on the right, and the hornets, emerging from St Saviour's 'to sting him', on the left. The vicar is hurrying for shelter in the parish church. (From Stephens, *Hook*, II, opp. p. 202)

of Anglicanism which is so often dismissed or underrated: the quiet, unaffected maintenance of tradition to keep the Church as a steady, dependable symbol of the importance of religion in the modern world. It is a type of Anglicanism which is not fashionable and far from spectacular, but is certainly not dead. It suggests that the Church of England has far more serious duties than to attract congregations by showy means and to attract publicity.'[33] In the challenging years of the twenty-first century the position of the Parish Church – now Leeds Minster – as a civic church, virtually a pro-cathedral, has been brought into question. In the 1970s it had faced possible closure but survived. The more recent disbandment of the boys' choir was another landmark – although the choral tradition has not only survived, but the newly-formed adult choir produces music of an outstanding quality, though daily sung evensong has ceased. If Leeds Minster has a role for the future it is surely as a place where the 'quiet, unaffected maintenance of tradition' is fused with a dynamic vision of the future as radical as was Hook's more than a century and a half ago.

Notes

1. Peter Leach and Nikolaus Pevsner, *The Buildings of England, Yorkshire West Riding, Leeds, Bradford and the North* (New Haven and London, 2009), 398–9.

2. W. R. W. Stephens, *The Life and Letters of Walter Farquhar Hook*, 2 vols (London, 1880), I, 371–2. However, all three were sufficiently well-attended to need the addition of substantial galleries in the 1830s. They were designed to contain galleries, but these had been omitted, as an economy, when the churches were constructed in the 1820s.

3. Stephens, *Hook*, I, 374.

4. Stephens, *Hook*, I, 405.

5. Stephens, *Hook*, I, 409. For a detailed account of work carried out to the church in the 18th century see T. Friedman, *Church Architecture in Leeds 1700–1799* (Leeds, 1996), 10–42. Ralph Thoresby described the church in 1715 as 'never so beautiful since its foundation'.

6. Stephens, *Hook*, 1, 380.

7. Stephens, *Hook*, II, 28. Rusby saw Hook as 'an old fashioned High Churchman' and concluded Hook had 'a distrust of the unhistorical ideas that characterised one section of the Oxford reformers'. James Rusby, *St Peters at Leeds, being an account historical and descriptive of the Parish Church* (Leeds, 1896), 67.

8. Nigel Yates, *Leeds and the Oxford Movement* (Leeds, 1975), 13.

9. *Leeds Intelligencer*, 20 January 1844. There were, in 1843, 1,095 services in total and 194 sermons preached.

10. Stephens, *Hook*, I, 390–1.

11. Stephens, *Hook*, 1, 175.

12. Rusby, *St Peters at Leeds*, 61. However, in the 1820s, the parish church held three services *every* day. Edward Baines, *History, Directory and Gazetteer of the County of York*, 2 vols (Leeds, 1822) I, 24.

13. Rusby, *St Peters*, 63.

14. *Leeds Intelligencer*, 30 November 1826; *Leeds Mercury*, 24 August 1826, *Leeds Mercury*, 24 November 1827. See also Paper 6 in this volume 'The Musical Tradition'.

15. See G. W. O. Addleshaw and F. Etchells, *The Architectural Setting of Anglican Worship* (London, 1948), 203 ff.

16. John Jebb, *The Choral Service of the United Church of England and Ireland* (London, 1843), 152.

17. Addleshaw and Etchells, *Architectural Setting*, 213.

18. *Leeds Mercury*, 27 April, 1837.

19. Stephens, *Hook*, I, 319.

20. West Yorkshire Archives Service, RDP 68/12/1.

21. R. W. Moore, *A History of the Parish Church of Leeds* (Leeds, 1877), 4–5. See also E. Kitson Clark, *A History and Description of St Peter's Church at Leeds* (London, n.d.), 7.

22. Stephens, *Hook*, II, 89.

23. Phoebe B. Stanton, *The Gothic Revival & American Church Architecture* (Baltimore, 1968), 33.

24. Yates, *Leeds*, 15.
25. Quoted in Dalton, 'Anglican Resurgence', 60.
26. *Leeds Intelligencer*, 3 December 1842.
27. *Leeds Intelligencer*, 14 October 1843.
28. Stephens, *Hook*, II, 197–8.
29. Yates, *Leeds*, 70–84 passim.
30. Yates, *Leeds*, 18–19.
31. Yates, *Leeds*, 19.
32. I am grateful to Simon Lindley, organist and Master of the Music at Leeds Parish Church from 1976 to 2016, for information on recent liturgical developments.
33. C. Moore, A. N. Wilson and G. Stamp, *The Church in Crisis* (London, 1986), 191.

4.

Class, Congregation and Community: Leeds Parish Church, 1841–1914

JANET DOUGLAS

The focus of this paper is the seemingly simple question of 'who sat in the pews', but for the historian the answer is far from clear-cut due to a paucity of evidence. Until recently social historians have concentrated their attention on three issues: how far was churchgoing largely a middle-class phenomenon, the relationships between the working classes and religion, and the decline of church attendance with the growth of secularism. Contemporary interests in broader issues of identity have raised questions about the role of women in religious life and, more radically, William Whyte has moved away from sociologically-inspired analysis to introduce a new paradigm to church history which directs attention to the experience of churchgoing and the sensory responses evoked by worship.[1] Informed by the emerging New Materialism, the centrality of human beings has been downgraded in favour of the affective capacities of the inanimate where, for example, the bricks and mortar are not to be considered passive but have their own competences to shape human experience and emotions.

For much of the nineteenth century the Anglican Church was on the defensive; the growth of industry and the rise of Nonconformity caused alarm in ecclesiastical circles. Associated with social privilege and political conservativism, the Church of England was imperilled to such a degree that when Hook arrived in Leeds in 1837, he wrote to a friend, 'the real fact is that the established church [here] is Methodism'.[2] In Leeds, Dissenters outnumbered Anglicans by 2 to 1. Leeds Parish Church appeared particularly vulnerable; the building itself was ramshackle, and was located amidst the worst slums in the town. Hook's mission was to augment his middle-class congregation whilst at the same time advancing his vocation to evangelise the urban poor who lived in the surrounding districts. To many of his contemporaries, he appeared to have accomplished both these possibly conflicting goals, and as a result Hook came to be regarded as 'one of the greatest and most successful parish priests in the country'.[3]

This paper considers the following issues: the 1851 Religious Census and church attendance at the Parish Church; the Parish Church and the Leeds middle classes; the Parish Church and initiatives to engage with the working classes; the feminisation of the church; the church as a civic institution; the experience of religious buildings and worship.[4]

The Religious Census and attendance at the Parish Church

On 30 March 1851, fourteen years after Hook's appointment, for the first and only time, there was a national census of religious worship. The results were regarded as deeply threatening to the Victorian middle-classes. Despite current scholars' criticisms of the census' methodology, its two broad findings are indisputable: most of the population attended neither church nor chapel; Nonconformity was thriving. In Leeds only 47 per cent of the population attended a place of worship on Census Sunday. Nevertheless, there were few empty pews at the Parish church; the morning service was attended by 1,800 and 2,800 were present at evening worship. According to the church wardens who compiled these figures, at least 350 people were obliged to stand during the evening service, and others were turned away. The new Parish Church had a total of 2,450 sittings, 1,000 more than in the old church. St Peter's had always had a substantial number of free places unlike Holy Trinity and St Paul's where there were none and St John's where there were very few, and Hook had insisted on increasing the number of free places to 1,800, all located in the nave of the church. The number of private pews was increased by 54. These were auctioned off, raising £3,649 for the church-building fund.[5] In total there were 650 appropriated sittings, all situated in the galleries. Appropriated pews were a commodity like any other, some pew owners never attended and rented out their places, the rental income going to the owners rather than the church. Advertisements even appeared in the local newspapers for the sale of pews.[6]

Hook's reputation as a powerful preacher undoubtedly inflated attendance figures at the Parish Church and 'church crawling' was a popular pastime as is attested by Benjamin Barker in his memoirs. The son of a Bramley cloth manufacturer, he was brought up 'with every possible prejudice against the Church' and as a young man spent his Sundays 'tasting' different sermons at various Nonconformist chapels. In 1852 he attended the special service at St Peter's to commemorate the death of the Duke of Wellington, 'this was the second or third time I had been at Leeds Parish Church and I was much pleased and impressed with the Church, the choral service, Dr Hook preached a very suitable sermon'. It was an epiphany moment for this young man and elsewhere in his recollections he notes that Hook was 'the greatest and most successful parish priest of the time'.[7] Preaching was widely regarded as the measure of the success of a minister and sermons were much discussed cultural events and might be reported in their entirety in the local newspapers.

It is difficult to know how far Dr Hook's 1859 departure from Leeds effected attendance at the Parish Church. Although there were some systematic surveys of church attendance in other parts of the country, no such local censuses were carried out in Leeds. Nationally, Anglican attendance appears to have fallen only slightly between 1851–81 but decline set in after 1881. The evidence we have for St Peter's is both anecdotal and contradictory. Fred Spark, the editor of the *Leeds Times* in his memoir reproduced an article he wrote in 1863, entitled 'Sunday Night at the Leeds Parish Church'.

> By twenty minutes past six o' clock the seats in the lower part of the church which are free, are full, but in the galleries there are few persons as yet, the pews there being private property, and the seats are reserved for the owners until the Psalms are sung. At half-past 6 the church is full … the occupants of the gallery seats have dropped in at the last minute, and it is surprising to see the studied indifference with which many of them appear to regard the service.[8]

Spark also noted that many of those seated in the galleries try to leave the church before the sermon and the vergers have resorted to the stratagem of barring the doors until the service was over. Eleven years later, however, Benjamin Barker found the church only half-full at the service to commemorate the anniversary of the consecration of St Peter's. Probably attendance fluctuated according to the time of the service, the ecclesiastical calendar and 'pulpit power'. Cosmo Lang, later Archbishop of Canterbury, who was a curate at the Parish Church, 1890–3, remembered one of his last sermons in Leeds when the church was so full that the congregation was crowded even onto the steps of the chancel.[9] His vicar, the Revd E. S. Talbot, was also a very fine preacher, 'He could hold the congregation to rapt attention. Rich were his cadences of his voice and shapely were the form of his sentences'.[10] The size of the congregations at the Parish Church was even commended in the national press; in 1897 the *Daily Mail* reporting that 'the building was packed from floor to galleries, with a congregation the like of which is not seen often.'[11] Yet the issue of the private gallery pews became an increasing problem for the church wardens and, in 1901, members of the congregation were rebuked for refusing to take vacant seats in the nave, and instead queued for unoccupied seats in the gallery: 'In the crush and struggle some people seemed to forget where they were.'[12]

The Parish Church and the Leeds middle classes

As we have seen, social distinctions were expressed in the seating arrangements of the Parish Church, a constant visual reminder of how status and social hierarchy were embedded into the very furniture and fittings of both churches and chapels. In a period when modern class identities were in the process of being constructed, the middle classes felt the need to distance themselves physically and culturally from working people whom they began to regard as rough and vulgar. Maintaining gentility and respectability, concepts integral to middle-class identity, meant that it was preferable to wait for empty gallery pews than sit amongst the poor in the nave! When Thomas Tennant, a Leeds merchant and later a Parish Church Trustee, was asked at a Parliamentary select committee in 1833 about what contact he had with the 'respectable' working class, his reply was revealing, 'I cannot say that I have had any communication with people of the description.'[13] Then as now, defining the middle class is problematic. R. J. Morris, a historian of nineteenth-century Leeds, has estimated that, at the very most, 25 per cent of the town's population might be classified as middle class, but within this class there were huge disparities of wealth and power. At the top of the social hierarchy was an elite of perhaps as few as 200 families whose annual incomes exceeded £1,000.[14] The stipend of the Vicar of Leeds of £1,257 placed men like Hook firmly within the ranks of the town's patricians. Morris speculates that amongst the Leeds elite there probably was a slight Anglican majority and he also noted that 80 per cent of Anglicans were Conservatives; amongst the more broadly defined middle class, the Established Church was a significant minority and there was far greater political pluralism.[15]

Of the micro-society of St Peter's, William Stephens, Hook's biographer, wrote 'there was never wanting a large number of men of wealth and influence' and he mentions a number of individuals whose names crop up over and over again in the annals of the Victorian Parish Church: men such as Henry Hall and his son, Robert, William and Christopher Beckett, John Hope Shaw, Thomas and Joseph Mason Tennant; of the latter, referring to his role on the building committee, Hook said 'Joe Tennant really built this parish church.'[16] At the pinnacle of the lay community, there were the Church Trustees, usually numbering 25, who were responsible for clerical appointments. When Hook was selected in 1837, ten of the trustees were woollen merchants. In addition, there were three bankers, three physicians, two lawyers and Griffiths Wright, the printer and the publisher of the Tory *Leeds Intelligencer*. Two-thirds of the trustees had been members of the old Corporation that was swept away by the Municipal Reform Act of 1835. All were Tories. These *grandees* were joined by a single manufacturer, J. R. Atkinson, the flax spinner. How far had the situation changed by 1891? Manufacturers now made up a third of the trustees, and only one woollen merchant survived, along with a phalanx of eight members of the older professions, plus an architect and a mining engineer. There were thirteen known Conservatives in 1891, two Liberal Unionists and a single Liberal Party supporter. The political allegiances of the remaining trustees are unknown. Next in the pecking order of social prestige at the Parish Church were the elected churchwardens. During the period when the churchwardens levied a church rate, elections might be contentious but by the 1850s church rates had largely disappeared and elections became a formality. The duties of a churchwarden were burdensome and, consequently, the social profile of churchwardens was far more heterogeneous than that of the trustees: men like William Gott, William Beckett-Denison and Joseph Mason Tennant might occupy this position as young men but, more generally, it was solicitors, bank managers, auctioneers, insurance agents and prosperous shop keepers who took up this role which certainly enhanced their standing in the local community.

Turning to pew owners, what is known of their social position? There is an extant list from 1841 giving the names of 170 pew owners and the sums they had paid for their pews. As one would expect, families like the Becketts, the Gotts, the Halls and the Tennants all had their own pews. The occupations of the vast majority covered a diversity of trades and professions: builders, wine merchants, printers, tobacconists, clerks and even a book clasp manufacturer. Some pew owners did not live in Leeds; the Willets, for example, lived in Shropshire and London. One problems with pews-as-property was that when an owner died, his pew might pass to a non-Leeds relative. And wills might be disputed: two members of the Hebdin family claimed Pew 24; Pew 96, worth £82, was claimed by Benjamin Hardwick Teale, Elizabeth Howarth and James Sigston. The former already owned another pew so we must deduce that it was not a sitting he wanted but the rental income.

For the middle classes, the Parish Church served a variety of functions, it was not only a place of worship and a badge of respectability, but also a centre for sociability and a vehicle for doing 'good works' for the wider community. This provided a plethora of activities for men and women and their families: Sunday school teaching; mothers meetings; ladies drawing room meetings; home visiting; the care of the sick and destitute; home mission work; and very importantly, fund

Fig. 4.1: The Leeds Middle Class School, Vernon Road, Woodhouse. Now part of Leeds University. (Thoresby Society Collection)

raising and bazaars. The dense social networks that flourished invaded both the council chamber and the boardroom: families inter-married and formed friendship groups which lasted through a lifetime.[16] Business opportunities were enhanced through what social scientists term 'a radius of trust', created through congregational intercourse and common values. For example, Charles Chorley (1830–1912), despite living in Headingley, was a churchwarden at St Peter's for 40 years, and acted as the church's in-house architect, building St Peter's School (with Dobson in 1856), the Church Middle Class School (1874–6), the Mission Church of the Good Shepherd (1882), the Meanwood Home for Waifs and Strays (1885), the Clergy House in 1888, the Market District Club (1908) besides numerous alterations and additions to the church itself.

An instance of the Parish Church's concern for its middle-class congregation was the founding in 1870 of the Leeds Church Middle Class School (Fig. 4.1). Spearheaded by the vicar, Dr Woodford, its purpose was to provide a secondary education for children of the middle-class parents who could not afford to send their sons and daughters to private schools nor pay the hefty fees of Leeds Grammar School (there was not yet a girls' high school). School bills at the LCMC varied from four to six guineas annually depending on the age of the pupil. Not only was the school affordable, but it provided 'a modern education', one that would appeal to parents whose livelihood was based in industry and commerce. Unlike the Grammar School which followed a traditional classical curriculum, science was integral to teaching at the LCMC along with modern languages such as French and German (Latin was an optional extra). The curates and occasionally the vicar from St Peter's were responsible for Scripture and Religious Instruction and though non-Anglican parents could withdraw their children from the latter, few did so.[17] The school was so successful that after six years it moved to purpose-built premises in Vernon Road where the building still stands. However, after the 1902 Education Act, pupil numbers began to decline, and the school closed in 1907.

Continued support from the middle classes

The question arises, why, after Hook's Vicarage Act, did the middle classes continue to patronise Leeds Parish Church? Suburbanisation meant that almost no middle-class families lived within the new parish of Leeds and there were some fine and far more convenient churches in the suburbs. What drew them to St Peter's? For some, they had family ties to the church going back into the eighteenth century, for the others it was the quality of the preaching, the music, and the splendours of the cathedral-style services. Leeds Parish Church remained a place of prestige within the local Anglican community, its staff 'formed a sort of aristocracy among the clergy of Leeds; a fact symbolised rather uncomfortably by the top hats and long black coats which they all wore!'[18] It attracted notable clerical figures as its vicars and, as Adrian Hastings noted, ambitious curates, who came 'down from Oxford for a stint of slumming before moving creditably on to greater ecclesiastical heights.'[19] St Peter's was (and still is) regarded as the mother church of the town and bestowed a self-regarding esteem on those associated with it. Finally, we need to consider how this middle-class congregation travelled to the Parish church. Certainly not all were 'carriage folk' and until the end of the century public transport was expensive and limited; we are left to presume that they walked from the suburbs like Woodhouse, Headingley, New Leeds and Chapel Allerton.[20]

The Parish Church and initiatives to engage the working classes

There was nothing new about the non-attendance of working people at church as many eighteenth century visitation records attest. What was different was that in the 1830s and 40s, the middle classes believed they were confronting an acute social crisis which might well overwhelm them. When James Smith visited Leeds in 1840 on behalf of the Royal Commission on the State of Large Towns, he argued that 'until the localities of the abodes of the working classes are rendered more approachable to the higher class of citizens, it is rash to expect that any useful intercourse can be maintained.'[21] The obstacles to cross-class relations were manifold, and graphically illustrated in the *Report of Town Mission* of 1849, 'in a street containing 50 families and 217 individuals, there are but 24 who attend public worship, there are 18 families without a bible, 39 adults unable to read, 18 drunkards and 5 houses of ill-fame.' Hook was only too aware of these problems adding that 'there is much hatred of the Church among working people as an aristocratic institution … the prevailing feeling among them is that all religion is humbug.'[22] In a sermon of 1846, he noted that less than 1 per cent of the working class attended a place of worship, 'the usual practice is for the men to lie in bed on Sunday morning, while the women cook the dinner and for an adjournment in the evening to take place in a public house.'[23] Despite such obstacles, Hook believed that it was his religious duty to try to bridge the gap between the social classes and bring the working classes to the Kingdom of God by Christian kindness. The middle class often equated 'the working class' and 'the poor', however the working class was as heterogeneous as the middle class and the class had its own hierarchy. At the top were skilled artisans, mechanics, millwrights, printers, and other craft workers in receipt of reasonable wages and who were in regular employment. Even amongst factory operatives, there was significant social differentiation dependent on levels of skill and responsibility. There were steady, respectable workers or, to quote Thomas Tennant again, 'the industrious part of the operatives who did not go into the beer shops.'[24] At the bottom of this ranking system were the labourers, the unskilled, seasonal workers who survived on the edge of destitution and often sank into it when trade was slack. The problem for Hook and the clergy who came after him was that the better-off workers increasingly did not live within the parish of Leeds. Like the middle class before them, they too had begun to move out of the crowded, degraded town centre, leaving St Peter's marooned amongst the masses of the indigent poor.[25]

Hook's ambition was to be regarded as 'the poor man's friend'. One reader of the *Leeds Intelligencer* described his work as 'indefatigable in the worst part of town, such as York Road and the Bank, where not many great, not many rich are found.'[26] Every morning at 10 am he was available to receive the poor at the vicarage (in Park Square) and he personally attended the fever sheds during the 1849 cholera outbreak. He visited the sick and dying in their own homes and, in times of poor trade, organised subscriptions and food kitchens at the Parish Church. His commitment to the Ten Hours movement was well-known in the town; at a huge meeting in 1844, to loud cheering, he declared that 'it was his duty as a vicar, to defend the weak against the strong … if ever a collision should come between the interests of the middle and working classes, he should take sides with the working class – because it was my first duty to preach the Gospel to the poor.'[27] Such was the extent of the trust placed in Hook by working men that during the 1858 West Yorkshire Coal Strike, the miners accepted Hook's offer to arbitrate in their dispute. Despite these sympathies and herculean labours, it is difficult to know how far Hook's endeavours had any lasting effects on church attendance though he undoubtedly left a legacy of goodwill amongst the wider community including Dissenters.[28] After he had left Leeds he wrote to his fellow cleric, F. W. Maurice, that thirty years ago, the workers hated the church but that 'it was different now at least in Yorkshire. The working classes respect Christianity though they stand aloof and only a few come to church.'[29]

Thirty years later, in 1874, one of Hook's successors, Dr John Gott (vicar, 1873–86), echoed many of Hook's concerns. At a Harvest Festival Service, he spoke about the 'religious wants of the masses and the best means of overtaking the vast spiritual destitution existing in Leeds.' The vicar declared that in Leeds 'there were 100,000 persons for whom no religious agencies existed, or who wilfully and uniformly disregarded if not scoffed, at all religion.' Drawing attention to 'the immorality and profaneness which are encountered at every stop in our dark alleys and overcrowded courts', he appealed to his congregation 'to make the self-sacrifice needful under these desperately urgent circumstances.'[30] Within a year of his appointment, Dr Gott had organised a week-long general mission involving clergymen from all over the country – it was the first general mission to be organised outside of London. Daily services were held in the churches, public meetings organised at the Church Institute and the Mechanics Institute, there were services in factories, some of which were attended by over a thousand men. A special mission was addressed to fallen women, and other meetings were held in Armley Gaol.[31] It was claimed that 40,000 attended the mission and eight years later, Gott arranged another general mission and a third was organised by Dr Talbot in February 1892 lasting ten days and involving 40 Anglican churches and 80 clergymen. This mission was planned on similar lines to the earlier ones with some innovations: there were three ecumenical services for businessmen in the Parish church, ten services for the working classes, three for women with special arrangements for child-care, and seven services for working men besides the numerous factory meetings. All seats in the Parish church were free during the mission.

Leeds Parish Church.

Good Shepherd Mission.

A.D. 1882–1932.

Fig. 4.2: The Good Shepherd Mission Church, erected 1882, closed 1932. It was demolished as part of the Quarry Hill slum clearance scheme. (Thoresby Society Collection)

The flyer promoting Talbot's mission implicitly revealed some of the problems the Anglican Church confronted in attracting male working-class participation in the church. 'Come to Mission each evening on Sundays at 6.30, or weekdays at 8pm. Come for a short service for working people every weekday at 1pm. Come, men, to Men's services on Sundays at 3pm. Come in your working clothes. Bring your friends. Sit where you please. Hymn books will be provided.'[32]

Clearly designed to allay any fears that individuals might have, the local press, including the often-critical *Leeds Mercury*, deemed the Mission to have been a great success but Dr Talbot was more doubtful. In a draft letter written in his hand and dated 27 March 1892, he wrote of his disappointment: 'In the recent Mission special efforts were made by workers clerical and lay to reach that class of men who inhabit the common lodging houses … every attempt discloses afresh the difficulty of reaching a class whose associations and surroundings are against them.' Undaunted, he suggested that what these men needed was 'some personal contact with those whose advantages have been greater than their own' and he issued an invitation to those interested in taking up this work to come to a meeting at the Church Institute.[33] Whether such a letter was ever sent we don't know, or perhaps Talbot's plea fell on deaf ears, but no meeting ever took place.

The Good Shepherd Mission

By their very nature, general missions could never establish a permanent presence in the town. Under Dr Woodford's ministry (1868–73), the church began to acquire empty houses in the parish to use as mission rooms, and Dr Gott, Woodford's successor, later divided the parish into four districts each with a senior curate in charge and a team of district visitors. The first mission house, the Good Shepherd, was acquired in 1870 in St Peter's Square. A young lay worker at the Parish Church, T. H. M. Brameld, a solicitor's clerk, described the area, 'The poverty of the people was desperate', and there was an enormous number of lodging houses, 'an open space next door to the mission rooms was referred to as the "Muck Yard", and the whole area was infested with vermin.'[34] A letter to the *Yorkshire Post* from the Parish Church curates confirmed this picture of squalor, 'immorality was openly practised, shameless solicitation, gambling in the streets and inadequate lighting.' There were, according to Dr Gott, 30 public houses in the area, eight in one street alone. However, mission services held at the Good Shepherd attracted substantial congregations of up to 200, people who would not have felt comfortable at St Peter's because they did not have Sunday clothes and the intellectual tone of the sermons was too demanding. In 1881 Dr Gott appealed for funds to build a permanent church in St Peter's Square: the Good Shepherd Mission. It was designed by Charles Chorley, cost £2,000 and was opened by Viscount Lascelles (Fig. 4.2). It is a measure of the success of this project that the church had to be enlarged twice. Sunday School attendances peaked at 700 and there was a wide range of recreational activities: cricket clubs, football, swimming, a gymnasium, and a seaside camping club. One of the curates, Tupper Carey, a close friend of Cosmo Lang, even persuaded the local publicans to allow him to talk to their clientele, gathering a group of about 40 men, who became known in the Clergy House as 'Tupper's burglars'.[35]

Other mission initiatives

The Book of the Arch describes another of the parochial mission projects.[36] It was situated in the arch of a railway viaduct and although only 250 yards from the Parish Church, clearly had a special attraction to some worshippers. Founded in 1895 by Edith Baines, the daughter of Frederick Baines, the editor of the *Leeds Mercury*, it was situated between Off Street and York Street (Fig. 4.3).[37] According to the Revd Hugh Marks, one of the two curates attached to the mission, 'the people in the district were at first amused by the idea and thought us slightly mad'. With trains rattling overhead, there was a Sunday service, a Wednesday evening service for women, and a men-only service

Fig. 4.3: The Arch Mission was founded in 1895. It was a room within one of the viaduct arches just to the left of the one in this photograph and behind the Lloyds Arms. The two sides of the arched space were bricked up to form the worship space. It could accommodate about 60 worshippers. It closed during the First World War but the viaduct itself – linking Leeds Station and Marsh Lane – is still extant. The Lloyds Arms was demolished in 1994.

Fig. 4.4: Arch Mission children at Saltburn (n.d.). (The Book of the Arch, Leeds City Libraries, Family and Local History Library)

every Friday with an average attendance of about twelve. The services for children were quite overwhelmed and many had to be sent away; according to the Revd Robert Shipman, appointed in 1901, 'the children were too ragged for the Good Shepherd'. The stories of these children are heart-rending. To give but two examples: a woman teacher took some children on a trip to Harewood, on the way she pointed to some

Fig. 4.5: Market District Boys Club football team (n.d.). (Postcard)

sheep and asked the children what they were. 'Appen they're wolves, miss' was the response of one little boy. On another occasion the Revd R. S. Medicott organised a visit to Bolton Abbey, and a pensive figure in black sat on the rock, gazing at the River Strid. When questioned about her thoughts, she replied 'how nice it would be to commit suicide, but she couldn't because the clothes she had on were borrowed' (Fig. 4.4). [38]

'Muscular Christianity' was another outreach strategy taken up by the Parish Church to attract working-class participation. The phrase, attributed to Charles Kingsley, refers to the attempt to tailor Anglicanism to a competitive and militaristic society, endorsing sport as a character-building activity. Taken up by many public schools and bearing in mind that most Anglican clergymen were public school boys, clerics soon appreciated that sport could be enrolled in the service of Christ and, as is well-known, some of our most famous football teams have their origins in church organisations.[39] The Leeds Parish Church Market District Boys Club was one such initiative. In 1889 two cottages in Harewood Street were rented to provide a boys' club to prevent lads roaming the streets. It advertised itself as offering 'football and fellowship', and soon a cricket team and a harriers' section (Figs 4.5, 4.6, 4.7). [40] By 1893 the club had 292 members.[41] Five years later, the arrival of the Revd O. M. Mackie was to herald a new chapter in the club's history. Mackie, born in Wakefield, was educated at Haileybury School and Clare College, Cambridge, but perhaps of greater significance was that he played rugby for Wakefield Trinity and England. A charismatic figure, under Mackie's tutelage, the club thrived and in 1901 moved to larger premises in Halliday Court, Kirkgate, where there were nine rooms including a large hall, a games room, a small chapel and baths in the basement, and a continuous supply of cocoa. 'Mackie gave you religion in the rough and you had to take it as it was given, but you loved the man,

Fig. 4.6: Football match poster, 1892.

Fig. 4.7: The Market District Boys' Club camping holiday (n.d.). (Thoresby Society Collection)

Fig. 4.8: The Market District Boys' Club, Marsh Lane, demolished in the 1990s. (Thoresby Society Collection)

you couldn't help it and that was everything.'[42] Some of the boys were even persuaded to attend the Parish Church where there was a special service for them every three weeks. By 1905 the Club was outgrowing its home in Kirkgate and the new vicar of Leeds, Samuel Bickersteth, approached the City Council for help with funding a new building to which the Corporation agreed on the condition that the facility was available to Nonconformists.[43] The new premises on Marsh Lane, costing £5,000, had lavish facilities which could accommodate 300 boys at any one time. It was open from 7–10pm each weekday evening and from 2–10pm on Saturdays (Fig. 4.8). There was a large gym, boxing ring, games rooms and a huge sunken bath big enough to accommodate 30 boys at a time. Mackie described the kind of boys the club sought to cater for as, 'Rough working-class lads that had nowhere to spend their evenings … the boys were at the mercy of roughs who would not work and did not want to work, and who were only too pleased to get hold of some lad to teach him to gamble.'[44] Having refused other clerical appointments, Mackie stayed for fifteen years finally leaving Leeds in 1913. Although club membership dipped slightly after his departure, the Market Club survived for another 70 years.

The evidence presented so far suggests that, except for its mission work, the Parish church failed to attract a substantial working-class congregation to services at St Peter's itself. If this was the case, then we are left with a conundrum. Who sat in the free pews in the nave? There are several possible answers to this question. Lower-middle-class individuals who could not afford pew rents had little choice but to accept the proximity of working people. Although the working classes who lived in the vicinity of St Peter's lived in squalor, there was also a respectable working class residing in places like Holbeck, Burley, Sheepscar and Burmantofts, all well within walking distance of the church. There is a tendency amongst historians to believe in the natural radicalism of the working classes, but workers' political affiliations were far more diverse. For example, the motto, 'the altar, the throne and the cottage' of the Leeds Conservative Operatives Society founded in 1835 (the first in the country) suggests that there was a popular conservatism that embraced Anglicanism. By 1838 the LCOS had 600 members, met weekly and had its own library of 300 volumes. Its leader was William Paul, a flax worker employed by Hives and Atkinson, earning £10 a year. We have already encountered Atkinson – he was the only one of the 1837 trustees who was a manufacturer. It was not unknown for employers to pressurise their employees to attend specific places of worship so this may well account for some of those who occupied the sittings in the nave. Another possible answer which will be discussed in more detail below is that nave seats were occupied by working-class women worshippers, and it is a sign of clerical prejudice that when commentators spoke of the absence of the working class, they were referring to working-class men.

Women and the Parish Church

Until recently, studies of nineteenth-century religion in Britain have totally disregarded gender as a subject worthy of scholarly enquiry which is surprising given that it has long been acknowledged that women vastly outnumbered men in terms of church attendance.[45] So serious was this imbalance that attempts were made to rectify it by establishing men-only services.[46] The Victorian ideal of 'the Angel in the House' had constructed a subordinate female identity that centred on dutiful domesticity, purity, notions of service and self-sacrifice.[47] It was also believed that women were endowed with unique moral and spiritual qualities, they were uncorrupted by the competitive public sphere occupied by men, and therefore had a special role, 'a civilising mission'. Anglican patriarchy upheld this gendered division of labour believing that it was divinely ordained.

An article by Jenny Jaggers, the feminist historian, begins with a quotation from Florence Nightingale writing in 1852. 'I would have given the Church my head, my heart, my hand. She would not have them … She told me to go back and do crochet in my mother's sewing room: or if I were tired of that, to marry and look well at the head of my husband's table. You may go to Sunday School if you like it, she said. But she gave me no training even for that. She gave me neither work to do for her, nor education for it.'[48] Marriage, however, was not an option for all women. The 1851 Census revealed that there were 365,000 unmarried women in Britain, many of whom would never marry not because they didn't choose to but because there was a still-unexplained imbalance between the numbers of women and men in society. With a lack of respectable alternatives, church-going women looked for opportunities to channel their energies into 'useful work' and were joined by some married women seeking to escape their confinement in the home. Such ambitions were not always welcomed; clergymen were often suspicious of their endeavours not only because of patriarchal tradition and theology, but having been educated in all-male public schools and universities, many had little experience of relating to women beyond the confines of home and family. To cite an example from Leeds, it was reported that the saintly but unmarried vicar, Dr Woodford, apparently had 'a constitutional shrinking from the other sex. He declared he couldn't understand them', and this even extended to confirmation classes when he would say to his curates, 'You take the girls, I can't make anything of them but give me the men and the boys.'[49]

However, the pastoral role of the church staked out by Dr Hook and his successors proved to be a boon for many Anglican women. The plethora of philanthropic activities far outstripped the supply of men able to take up voluntary work on this scale and it could only be sustained by the enrolment of women. Church philanthropy was a field in which women could exercise their altruism, liberating themselves in the process. Rapidly they became the backbone of parish activity: home visiting, Bible classes, mothers' meetings, mission work both at home and overseas, educational activities, clothing clubs and saving banks, temperance campaigns and, later in the century, campaigns for social purity. In most instances, women worked under the supervision of men but particularly where 'women's issues' were concerned, they could operate more autonomously. Also regarded as women's work were fund raising bazaars; though men frequently opened the bazaars, this was usually the limit of their involvement. Bazaars were more elaborate affairs than we might imagine today, lasting for up to a week often with lavish themed decorations.[50] From the 1890s onwards even the numbers of male Anglican Sunday School teachers began to decline. Across the whole of Leeds, in 1893 there were 769 men to 1,407 women and by 1904 there were more than twice as many women as men. A sign of the important role women played in the life of the church came about when the Leeds Institute established a women-only club room in 1901.

An example of an exclusive Anglican organisation run by women was the Girls Friendly Society founded in 1875 by Mary Elizabeth Templeton to bring together ladies and working girls for mutual help in leading pure and useful lives. Its specific concern was to protect working class girls from rural areas who arrived in towns to find employment and were subject to all kinds of temptations. The Leeds branch of the society began with a meeting in the Philosophical Hall in January 1881 presided over by Dr Gott. The vicar made it clear that he believed that such an organisation was part of the ministry of the Anglican Church in Leeds, and Mrs Templeton who addressed the meeting, referred to the society as 'the handmaiden of the Church'.[51] 'Working' members, called 'associates' of the GFS, had to be Anglicans but 'ordinary' members, the recipients of aid, did not, though they were encouraged to attend church. Within a year the Leeds branch had 31 working members, 49 supporting members and 293 ordinary members and three years later it established its first lodge at 8 Upper Fountaine Street, with a kitchen, living room, recreation and meeting rooms and several bedrooms.[52] Other activities included patrolling the railways stations on the lookout for vulnerable young women, the establishment of an employment register and fund-raising to support holiday lodges in Scarborough and Filey. The GFS still exists and has branches throughout the world. Rather similar concerns motivated Emily Ford, a close friend of Dr Talbot, to buy the old clergy house in Kirkgate and convert it into a women's club for working girls open from 3–10pm on weekdays and all day on Sundays with cheap meals available for club members.[53]

As women's involvement in organisations grew so did their competencies and confidence, and a tension emerged between their experience of female autonomy and clerical control of women's work. This female subordination was manifest by their lack of any formal representation in the councils of the Church either nationally or locally. At Church Congresses for example, women might be admitted but were not allowed to speak despite their central role in parochial activities. Although both High Church and Evangelical clerics tended to be wary of any moves towards gender equality, women's grievances were sharpened as the women's suffrage movement gained momentum towards the end of the nineteenth century.[54] It comes as no surprise that most Anglicans were opposed to women's suffrage but in 1909 the Revd Claude Hinscliffe founded the Church League for Women's Suffrage; 'Votes for Women' was becoming a holy war based on spiritual imperatives and the equality of men and women before God. In November 1913 there was even 'a suffragette incident' in the Parish Church when, during a service, two young women shouted suffragette slogans (Fig. 4.9). They were not ejected and at the end of the service were able to hand out pamphlets to the congregation.[55] The organisational affiliations of the two women is unknown but by 1914 the CLWS had 103 branches and 5,000 members including 500 Anglican clergymen. Having trawled through the local newspapers, no mention of a Leeds branch has been found, but there was one. Indeed, the Northern Organiser for the League was based in Leeds. The CLWS's monthly journal, *The Church Militant*, recorded that in June 1914 a drawing room meeting was held to establish a branch in Leeds, and there followed a 'splendid meeting', held in St Saviour's Parish Rooms. 'The room was packed with enthusiastic people, 12 new members joined, and 70 copies of the paper were sold along with badges and other literature. Members stayed behind after tea to appoint the committee.'[56] The Branch President was a prebendary of the Ripon Diocese, and the Secretary was Miss Marjory Palmer of Newton Priory, Chapeltown Road, Leeds. Although the primary objective of the League was to secure the franchise for women, members of the CLWS were not blind to the links between this goal and the position of women in the Church itself. In May 1915 for example there was a large audience

Fig. 4.9: Church Women's League for Women's Suffrage, membership badge.

for a CLWS meeting in Leeds to discuss 'The Question of Women and Church Councils'. In 1920 the Lambeth Palace Conference debated the restoration of a diaconate for women, one speaker representing the Ripon Diocese pointed out that 'women were more successful in raising money for church purposes.'[57] The *Yorkshire Post* interviewed several women in Leeds about the matter. A prominent, but anonymous, church woman welcomed the proposal, calling it 'a measure of tardy justice'. Miss Baines also expressed her approval of the increased recognition of women's usefulness in the councils of the church and pointed out that 'for a great many years, women had done the most valuable work for the church and obviously as church workers, their presence must be advantageous'. The final word must go to Emily Ford, a Quaker who converted to Anglicanism: 'in my view laywomen ought to have exactly the same recognition in the church as a layman and I very much resent laymen preaching if women can't. I feel very strongly about this matter because women as a rule do a good deal more work for the Church than men do.'[58]

The civic role of the Parish Church

Throughout the Georgian period, each substantial town would designate one of its churches as the civic church where the mayor, aldermen and magistrates would assemble on Sundays accompanied by conspicuous ceremonial. As elsewhere prior to 1835, Leeds Corporation had been an exclusively Tory and Anglican body and as was customary, the mayor and the corporation had their own pews in the nave symbolising the union of church and state. These mutual interests were shattered by the Municipal Reform Act; overnight Tory control was replaced by a thumping Liberal Party majority and most, though not all, Liberals were Nonconformists. The first mayor of the reformed corporation was George Goodman, a Baptist, followed by T. W. Tottie, a Unitarian. In 1838 the councillors even elected James Holdforth, a Roman Catholic – the first Catholic to hold mayoral office since the Reformation. There was not to be an Anglican mayor until 1848 when John Hope Shaw, a Liberal, was elected. It was Goodman who, in 1836, set out the parameters for municipal/church relations: he declined to attend church every Sunday with the town mace and a train of municipal officers and announced that he would go to St Peter's only on special occasions accompanied by those members of the council who *wished* to attend.[59] What constituted 'a special occasion' was left to the mayor and, of course, was dependent on a formal invitation from the vicar.[60] Despite the rancorous political conflicts between the Church and the Corporation in the 1840s, and some sniping from Edward Baines junior in the *Leeds Mercury* and the *Leeds Times*, Goodman's compromise appears to have prevailed throughout the rest of the nineteenth century.[61]

The first important test case came in 1838 with the coronation of Queen Victoria, undoubtedly 'special'. Nevertheless, Mayor Tottie called a public meeting which, according to the *Leeds Mercury*, no Tories attended.[62] Tottie reflected on the coronation of William IV when the mayor and the council had attended the Parish church, and Tottie announced that he intended to do the same except that the Parish church was in the process of being rebuilt so the coronation service was to be held at St John's. The *Leeds Mercury* thundered its opposition, 'Our worthy mayor who seems to us to have greater reverence for the old, closed Tory corporation than they deserve … we see no reason at all that Dissenters of various denominations should be asked to go to the Parish Church and more especially that church where they are continually abused as schematics with whom churchmen ought to hold no religious communion.'[63] Nevertheless, on 30 June 1838 the mace holder headed a procession of the mayor with his gold chain and cocked hat, six aldermen, but only ten (out of 64) councillors, and various municipal officers. They walked from the Court House in Park Row to St John's Church and after the service, the mayor publicly subscribed to the Parish Church Building Fund as a mark of respect to the Church. Following the service, the civic pageant then proceeded to Hunslet Moor and, according to the *Leeds Mercury,* it was an impressive event,[64] although the *Leeds Times* reported it rather differently, 'this trashy ceremony [was] an object of wonder to the gaping crowd to those vulgar propensities to whom these rara-shows always appeal.'[65]

Spectacles such as this cemented local identification and made visible the links between the Church and the town. These early Dissenter mayors maintained that it was their civic duty to attend such events, but the absence of many of the town councillors even at a coronation service showed that not all corporation members were in agreement, believing that this compromise privileged one religious denomination over others. Despite these snubs, when Dr Hook rebuilt the Parish church, he provided a set of pews opposite the pulpit for the mayor and corporation for use on specific occasions such as memorial services for local dignitaries and national politicians, sermons preached on behalf of the Infirmary and the Public Dispensary and thanksgiving services following military successes, though always with an opt-out clause for those councillors whose Nonconformist consciences barred their attendance.

This détente was occasionally challenged on the Liberal/ Nonconformist side. For example, there was a great agitation in 1862 when James Kitson, mayor between 1861 and 1862, attended the Parish church without the insignia of his office, apparently infringing a corporation byelaw based on the notion that on occasions like this, the mayor was a public figure, not a private individual and should dress appropriately. Kitson's response to this attack was to defend himself on the grounds of religious equality, maintaining that he would not be party to a practice which permitted the civic insignia to be taken to one denomination but not to others.[66]

Clearly, Nonconformist hostility to the Church of England survived well into the second half of the nineteenth century – for example in 1872, when the Anglican Church announced that the Twelfth Church Congress would take place in Leeds and the Town Council was invited to take part in the opening procession. Although Church Congresses were prestigious affairs that would be reported in the national press, for the Corporation the event created a dilemma: civic pride versus Nonconformist conscience. The current mayor, John Barran, a Baptist, called a special council meeting to discuss what he recognised would be a divisive invitation. Indicating from the beginning that he was in favour of accepting the invitation, the objections varied from the trivial to the principled: Robert Addyman pointed out that the procession clashed with market day in Leeds, others like Robert Meek Carter and Thomas Tatham believed it was unwise to give official sanction to any one religious denomination that could create a bad precedent. The more pragmatic argued that it would be embarrassing if only a few councillors participated so better decline rather than dishonour. Barran refused to allow a vote to be taken and reiterated the view that participation was entirely optional.[67] On 8 October, the Mayor and members of the corporation, 'a goodly number', according to the *Leeds Times*, left the Town Hall to join the main procession at the Church Institute before proceeding to the Parish church.[68]

Nineteen years later, St Peter's celebrated its golden jubilee attended by the Archbishop of Canterbury, and Dr Talbot invited the Town Council to attend the Parish church on Sunday, 12 July 1891 when the Archbishop would preach. There were no reported objections to the Corporation's involvement in this ceremony. Municipal quibbles about such a prestigious occasion had clearly become unthinkable. The streets were decorated and lined with spectators as over 100 clergymen marched through the town amidst flags, banners, and bands. In their midst was the Archbishop Benson with his mitre, crozier and long train carried by Dr Talbot's two small sons. According to the *Yorkshire Post*, 'the animation in the streets … indicate the affection for the mother church which 't'owd Vicar [Dr Hook], in days gone, instilled into the hearts of the people of Leeds.'[69] A week later the *Leeds Mercury* conceded that, 'taken as a whole, the record of the last fifty years has been a splendid one. The church has become the centre of civic life. She is set on a hill and it is impossible for the most careless to ignore her presence or be wholly ignorant of her principles. The example of pastoral work, of reverence and splendour of worship, of effective organisation which men have seen in the parish church, has had an influence not only on the whole town but in the whole country … We have had enough of division, we now need association and combination of effort.'[70]

The power of place: experiencing the Parish Church

The question 'who sat in the pews' has so far been examined through the lens of historical sociology. An alternative approach championed by William Whyte focuses on the experience of churchgoing. While acknowledging the difficulties of capturing past experiences, Whyte has argued that architecture, decoration, and liturgical practices each have their own agency which together act upon both the senses and the emotions.[71] Before the 1830s, public worship in England was comparatively dull, plain and unceremonial which perhaps explains why, when Hook arrived in Leeds, he found St Peter's in such a pitiful condition, with only 50 communicants, mostly old women, and services were often garbled or else abandoned because attendance was so meagre.[72] Hook's incumbency was to transform Leeds Anglicanism. As well as the rebuilding the Parish church, he introduced cathedral-type services with a robed choir, choral settings of services and sublime church music. The contrast between these splendours and the drab environment in which many people lived could not have been greater. External appearances matter, they emit their own aura which Hook recognised: the exterior of St Peter's must be handsome both to impress and perhaps entice passers-by. The Gothic Revival thus became a weapon in the battle for souls and if imitation is the sincerest form of flattery, it helped push the Nonconformists all over Britain to adopt Neo-Gothic for their own buildings in an effort to compete with a resurgent Anglicanism.[73]

Consequently, along with his powerful preaching, Hook and his new church provided his congregation with a 'total experience': a church, according to Hook, was a kind of 'standing sermon'[74] within which both eyes and ears were beguiled by extravagant ornamentation, colour and glorious sounds. Worship became a sacred theatre through which the congregation might encounter the Divine. Such visual enchantment was believed to be particularly important in missionary work amongst the toiling masses because it acted as a counterfoil to the dreariness of their lives. 'Ritualism' according to Richard Littledale, a nineteenth-century cleric, 'was vital in mounting a challenge to the splendours of the gin palaces in which internal decoration, abundant polished metal and vivid colour with plenty of bright light, is found to pay and to induce the people to stay on drinking, just because everything is so pretty and cheerful to the eye and so unlike the squalid discomfort of their own sordid homes.'[75] Hook too believed that the working class was starved of visual delight and might be brought closer to God by setting before them a loveliness that might induce a sense of rapture. After 1841 he ensured that St Peter's was open during the day to furnish 'a place of beauty and stillness in which they could escape from their crowded homes for private prayer and meditation.' [76] Hook's hopes probably fell on stony ground; the obstacles 'to dropping into' the Parish Church were insurmountable for most working people and the intoxication provided by religious worship was never going to successfully compete with the pleasures of the public house.

Concluding remarks

Any historian is the prisoner of the available primary sources, though we also need to remember that evidence needs to be sifted and interpreted. What, for example, are we to make of the 1903 statement of the Revd Gibson that the offertories at the Parish church now contained 'far more copper' than twenty years ago?[77] The *Leeds Mercury*, not always a friend of the Established Church, stated in 1903 that the pews were still well-filled, so does this mean that the well-to-do had retained their loyalty to the Parish Church but had become more niggardly, or else had they withdrawn to their suburban churches to be replaced by poorer working-class worshippers? Without further evidence, we simply do not know.

When Dr Hook arrived in Leeds in 1837, he found a town that was a fortress of Dissent and where Anglicanism was virtually moribund. Hook's achievement was to rehabilitate the Church of England in the town by his insistence of its relevance to an industrial society. Although the evidence is far from conclusive, it remains doubtful whether his efforts and those of his successors entirely won the allegiance of the working classes, particularly the poor who lived in the environs of the Parish Church. Perhaps what he and his successors did win was their respect and in some cases their affection which meant that those who did worship at St Peter's or one of its mission churches were not shunned by their neighbours. What must have been the familiar sight of Hook and his curates walking the streets of their adopted town resulted in the Parish Church becoming deeply embedded in the social fabric of Leeds. Forty or so years later, in the *Leeds Mercury* article, cited above, the reporter implies that this was still the case, maintaining that evening services at the Parish church attracted persons of all denominations and even those with no denominational commitment, all of whom were drawn by the forceful preaching and the musical excellence of the services.

In the years immediately following the First World War, a 1922 letter to the *Yorkshire Post* implies that St Peter's was still attracting large congregations, but this had changed by 1938 when the vicar, Thompson Elliot, claimed the decline in church attendance was due to the slum clearances around the Parish Church.[78] His comments might suggest that the middle classes had deserted the Parish Church, and that by the 1930s St Peter's was reliant on a lower middle/working class congregation, although such was the status of the Parish Church that it continued to attract the wealthier members of Leeds society. Elliot's comments exemplify the status of the Parish Church in the city: its 'function ... is not commensurate with the number of people who attend ... [but] it bears witness to the faith and work of the Church in the heart of this great Industrial city.' Bearing witness to this 'work', Dr Hook's statue still stands in City Square (see Fig. 5.1). Those who pass it by probably have little idea who he was or why he is there but do recognise that he is honoured as a 'Leeds Worthy' and a part of shared local identity.[79]

Notes

1. William Whyte, *Unlocking the Church* (Oxford, 2017).
2. W. R. W. Stephens, *The Life and Letters of Walter Farquhar Hook*, 2 vols (London, 1879), I, 406.
3. Quoted in Douglas A. Reid, 'Playing and Praying' in M. Daunton (ed.), *The Cambridge Urban History Of Britain* (Cambridge, 2000), 786.
4. For limitations of space I am not discussing Sunday Schools or the role of the Anglican Church in the provision of public education.
5. The most expensive pew was sold to the solicitor, Robert Barr for £200 and the cheapest, a pew at the back of the north gallery with an obstructed view of the altar, raised a paltry £15.
6. In 1870 for example, Pew No. 37 with five sittings was advertised for sale in the *Yorkshire Post*, 7 December 1869.
7. Benjamin Barker's Diary and Papers, Leeds, Thoresby Society Archives, MS Box X1.
8. Fred R. Spark, *Memories of My Life* (Leeds, 1913), 126–9.
9. J. G. Lockhart, *Cosmo Gordon Lang* (London, 1949), 100.
10. Quoted in Lockhart, *Lang*, 94
11. Quoted in the *Leeds Times*, 25 September 1897.
12. *Yorkshire Evening Post*, 11 April 1901.
13. R. J. Morris, *Class, Sect and Party: The Making of the British Middle Class: Leeds 1820–50*, (Manchester, 1990), 163.
14. R. J. Morris, *Men, Women and Property in England 1780–1870*, (Cambridge, 2005), 42.
15. Morris, *Class*, 320.
16. Stephens, *Hook*, II, 325–6.
17. For example, in 1829 Henry Hall's only son, Robert, married Maria Tennant, the second daughter of Thomas Tennant About a quarter of the pupils were from Non-conformist backgrounds. See E. Kilburn Scott, *Leeds Church Middle Class School* (Leeds, 1927).
18. Gwendolen Stephenson, *Edward Stuart Talbot* (London, 1936), 72.
19. Adrian Hastings, 'The Role of Leeds in English Religious History' in A. Mason (ed), *Religion in Leeds* (Stroud, 1994), p. 8. Apparently, a common saying in Anglican circles was 'Vicars of Leeds don't die, they translate'.
20. New Leeds is now better known today as Chapeltown. The vicarage was in Park Square until 1873, moving firstly to Denison Hall and then Hillary Place in Woodhouse.
21. Kitson Clarke, *Leeds University Review*, vol. 17, no 2, 1974, 232–58.
22. Stephens, *Hook*, II, 496.
23. Patricia Midgely, *The Churches and the Working Classes*, (Cambridge, 2012), 38.
24. Morris, *Class*, p. 164.
25. The Leeds Vicarage Act (1844) divided the huge parish of Leeds. See Dr Hammond's paper in this publication.
26. *Leeds Intelligencer*, 31 October 1840.
27. H. W. Dalton, 'Walter Farquhar Hook, Vicar of Leeds: his work for the Church the Town 1837–48', *Publications of the Thoresby Society*, Vol LXIII, 1990, 78.

28. Dalton, 'Hook', 76–9

29. J. F. C. Harrison, *Learning & Living 1790–1960* (London, 1961), 161.

30. *Leeds Times*, 19 September 1874.

31. Midgley, *Churches*, pp. 69–70; Roy Yates, 'Church and Town: the ministry of John Gott as Vicar of Leeds' in *The Local Historian*, vol. 17, no 1, 2017, 59–60.

32. West Yorkshire Archives, Leeds Parish Church Mission Scrapbook, 1892, RDP 68/112/3.

33. West Yorkshire Archive Service, Leeds Parish Church Mission Scrapbook, 1891, RDP68/112/3.

34. *The Good Shepherd Mission 1882–1932*, (probably Leeds, but not stated, 1932).

35. *The Good Shepherd Mission*, 17.

36. There were also mission halls in Harewood Street, Holdforth Square, and Halliday Court, off Kirkgate.

37. Leeds Library Services, Family and Local Studies Library, *The Book of the Arch* (1920) LP269 LS17. The Baines family were prominent Congregationalists and stalwart upholders of Non-conformity, but Edith Baines joined the Established Church in the early 1890s under the spiritual guidance of Dr Talbot.

38. *The Book of the Arch*, 10.

39. For example, Everton, Fulham, Manchester City, Southampton, Aston Villa

40. Harriers engaged in a form of cross-country running.

41. *Leeds Mercury*, 3 June 1893.

42. Thoresby Society Library, *The Market District Boys Club 1889–1963*, class mark 523.3.

43. Midgley, *Churches*, 218.

44. *Yorkshire Post*, 17 January 1908.

45. In a *Daily News* survey of religious attendance in West London, November 1902, women formed 69 per cent those attending Anglican services.

46. Even before the appointment of Dr Hook, it was noted that whilst there were only 50 communicants at St Peter's '*nearly all women*'. Sheridan Gilley, 'Walter Farquhar Hook' in Mason, *Religion in Leeds*, 55.

47. *The Angel in the House* is the title of a poem written by Coventry Patmore in 1854.

48. Jenny Jaggers, 'The Victorian Female Civilising Mission and Women's Aspirations towards the Priesthood in the Church of England', *Women's History Review*, vol. 10, no. 4, 2001, 651.

49. C. G. Lang, *Church and Town for Fifty Years* (Leeds, 1891), 22.

50. Simon Morgan, *A Victorian's Woman's Place: Public Culture in the 19th Century*, (Manchester, 2007), chapters 5 and 6.

51. *Yorkshire Post*, 15 October 1881.

52. The Lodge was opened by the Bishop of Ripon. *Leeds Times*, 20 September 1884.

53. *Leeds Times*, 19 October 1895.

54. Many High Church clerics were in favour of Anglican sisterhoods, the first of which was established in 1845 and by 1900 the number of Anglican sisters had risen to between 2 and 3,000. Although Dr Pusey had written

to Dr Hook in 1839 suggesting the establishment of a sisterhood in Leeds, Hook who was trying to distance himself from 'Romanish' practices, didn't take up Pusey's suggestion which later bore fruit when Mother Agnes Stewart came to Leeds in 1871 attached not to the Parish church, but St Saviour's.

55. *Yorkshire Post*, 17 November 1913; *Yorkshire Evening Post*, 17 November 1913.

56. *Church Militant*, 1 July 1914.

57. Although there was no deaconess at the Parish church until the 1930s, the first Anglican deaconess in England was appointed in 1862 and by 1919, 431 women had been ordained as deaconesses, none of whom were in the Diocese of Ripon.

58. *Yorkshire Post*, 18 August 1920.

59. *Kendal Mercury*, 3 January 1836.

60. There is some evidence that not all Anglicans welcomed Dissenters into their Church, e.g. *Leeds Mercury*, 16 June 1838.

61. For details of these conflicts see Harry W. Dalton, 'The Anglican Resurgence under W. F. Hook', *Publications of the Thoresby Society*, vol. 12, 2002, 129–41.

62. *Leeds Mercury*, 16 June 1838.

63. *Leeds Mercury*, 16 June 1838.

64. *Leeds Mercury*, 30 June 1838.

65. *Leeds Times*, 9 June 1838, 30 June 1838.

66. *Leeds Mercury*, 11 November 1862; *Leeds Intelligencer*, 11 November 1862; *Leeds Times*, 16 November 1862.

67. *Yorkshire Post*, 1 October 1872; *Leeds Mercury*, 1 October 1872.

68. *Leeds Times*, 12 October 1872.

69. *Yorkshire Post*, 13 July 1891.

70. *Leeds Mercury*, 23 July 1891.

71. Whyte, *Unlocking*, chapters 1 and 2.

72. Nigel Yates, 'Religious Life in Leeds' in D. Fraser (ed.), *A History of modern Leeds*, (Manchester, 1980), p. 254.

73. In Leeds, the Unitarians of Mill Hill were quick off the mark. Their rebuilt chapel of 1847 designed by Henry Bowman, was Gothic both in style and plan.

74. *Leeds Intelligencer*, 11 November 1837.

75. Quoted in Dominic James, *Victorian Reformation: The Fight over Idolatry in the Church of England, 1840–60* (Oxford, 2009), 36.

76. Dalton, 'Anglican Resurgence', 72.

77. Leeds Mercury, 17 April 1903; *Yorkshire Post*, 17 April 1903; *Yorkshire Evening Post*, 16 April 1903.

78. *Yorkshire Post*, 13 January 1922; *Yorkshire Post*, 26 April 1938.

79. City Square was the brainchild of T. Walter Harding who was responsible for the choice of the statues located in the square. Harding was an Anglican who worshipped at the Parish church, his father was a church trustee. The statue was the work of F. W. Pomeroy, a significant British sculptor.

5.

'For every poor man a pastor and for every poor child a school': Dr Hook's Building Enterprises

CHRISTOPHER HAMMOND

In City Square, close to the former Post Office, stand four statues of men pre-eminent in the history and development of Leeds: John Harrison, a Royalist in the time of the Commonwealth, founder of St John's Church, Alms houses and re-builder of Leeds Grammar School; Joseph Priestley,

Fig. 5.1: Dr Hook by Frederick William Pomeroy, bronze, 1898–1903. (Charlotte Winn)

discoverer of oxygen and Minister at Mill Hill Chapel; James Watt, albeit of no direct connection with Leeds, but whose improvements with the steam engine contributed to Leeds' industrial prosperity. The fourth is of Dr Walter Farquhar Hook, Vicar of Leeds, 1837–59. This statue (Fig. 5.1), donated by Colonel T. W. Harding, sculpted by F. W. Pomeroy and erected around 1900, shows Hook, one hand clasping a prayer book, the other raised in blessing. It is fitting that Hook's statue should be here rather than outside the Parish Church because his influence in educational, social and economic reform extended across the whole town. Fitting too that he should be holding a prayer book, the source of his faith in 'Church Principles', the *via media* of the Anglican Church.

Hook's statue, erected some forty years after the end of his ministry in Leeds, is also a testimony to his abiding influence in the life and work of the city, and the esteem with which he is held to the present day. Although Hook's achievements were many as he sought to improve the moral and material welfare – as well as the working and living conditions – of his parishioners, this paper focuses on his ambitious schemes to erect more churches and schools in the expanding town, one growing rapidly as a range of thriving industries drew in ever more workers. It is a story of determination to revitalize the Church of England in the town, but also one of personal generosity, careful analysis of problems, endless fundraising and tireless energy. When he left Leeds in 1859, the Church was in an infinitely better position than when he arrived. Anglicans in Leeds had cause to be exceedingly grateful for his vision, yet many of the buildings he worked tirelessly to fund had only limited life-spans.

The Revd Mr Hook was instituted as Vicar of Leeds on 4 April 1837, a few weeks before the conferment of Doctor of Divinity at Oxford (20 May) following which he preached twice at the University Church of St Mary 'thronged with an immense crowd up to the very steps of the pulpit'.[1] Perhaps he realised then that the existing church provision in Leeds was going to be entirely inadequate for his new ministry.

Church provision in the parish of Leeds in 1837

When Hook arrived in Leeds, the huge parish – some 30 miles in circumference – comprised the in-township and ten out-townships (Map 5.1). The in-township was served, in addition to the Parish Church, by the following seven churches which had the status of chapels of ease: St John the Evangelist, New Briggate (1634); Holy Trinity, Boar Lane (William Etty, 1722–7); St Paul, Park Square (William Johnson, 1791–3, dem. 1936); St James, York Street (1801, dem. *c.*1900);[2] St Mary, Quarry Hill (Thomas Taylor, 1823–6, dem. *c.*1980); Christ Church, Meadow Lane (R. D. Chantrell, 1821–6, dem. 1975); St Mark,

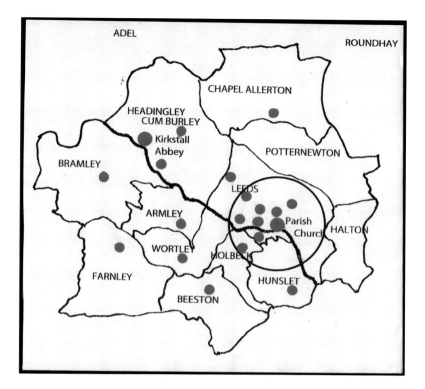

Map 5.1: The ancient parish or borough of Leeds showing the township boundaries and the sites of the chapels of ease existing in 1837, indicated by red dots. The circle is of 1-mile radius centred on the Parish Church.

Woodhouse (Atkinson & Sharp, 1823–6). An eighth, St George, Mount Pleasant (John Clark, 1836–8), was in the process of being built.

In 1837, the out-townships were served by the following ten chapels of ease: Armley, St Bartholomew (ancient, extended 1820s); Beeston, St Mary (ancient, enlarged 1790); Bramley, St Margaret (18th century, extended 1830s); Chapel Allerton, St Matthew (ancient, subsequent extensions); Farnley, St Michael and All Angels (John Carr, c.1761); Headingley, St Michael and All Angels (ancient, replaced, R. D. Chantrell, 1836–8); Holbeck, St Matthew (ancient, replaced, R. D. Chantrell, 1827–32); Hunslet, St Mary the Virgin (c.1636, enlarged 1744 and 1820s); Kirkstall, St Stephen (R. D. Chantrell, 1827–9); St John the Evangelist, Wortley (1813).[3]

The Leeds in-township, in which the Parish Church was situated, was by far the most populous, exceeding that of all the out-townships together. The census of 1841, the year of the consecration of St Peter, revealed the population of the Leeds in-township was 88,741 and of the out-townships 63,313.[4] Indeed, with the rapidly increasing urbanisation in the nineteenth century, the old township boundaries began to lose their physical significance 'on the ground'. The population distribution is better represented by a circle of one mile radius, centered on the

Parish Church (Map 5.2) enclosing an area of some 3.4 square miles. This includes Hunslet to the South East, Holbeck to the South West, Little Woodhouse to the West, Little London to the North West and Quarry Hill to the East. As will be noted later, it is within, or just outside this area, that all but one of the new churches erected during Hook's vicariate were subsequently demolished.

Anglican provision of seats per head of population in the out-townships may be roughly estimated from the total number of seats in the ten chapels of ease, listed above. Assuming a bench-mark figure of 400 for each chapel, the total number of seats, 4,000, provided accommodation for about 6 per cent of the population, considerably less than the 16.1 per cent provision for the Leeds in-township.[5]

Of the seven churches in the in-township, three (Holy Trinity, St Paul and St James) contained no free seats and were open only to those who could afford pew rents – the poor were effectively excluded. At this time, almost all churches and chapels contained some rented pews as an essential source of income, but in these three, there was sufficient demand for rented pews for the churches to contain nothing else. And a church with no free seats provided a degree of exclusivity to its genteel

Map 5.2: Church provision in Leeds in 1859 when Hook left Leeds, based on a map by J. Rapkin of 1850. The circle is of 1-mile radius, centred on the Parish church. The red dots represent demolished churches. Only Leeds Parish Church, St George and St Saviour – represented by green dots – have survived. All the Hook churches beyond the 1-mile radius and not shown on this map – St Thomas, Stanningley, Holy Trinity, Meanwood, St John the Evangelist, Moor Allerton and St Matthias, Burley – are extant.

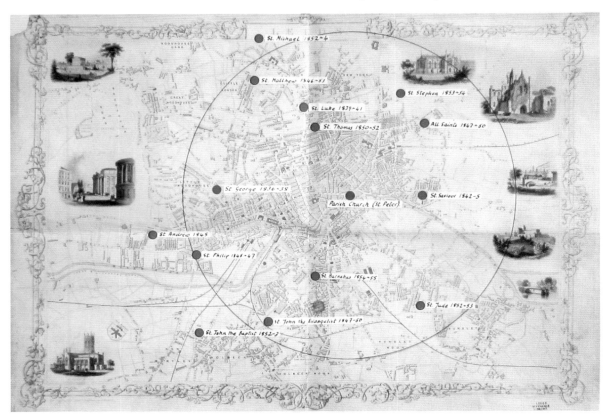

worshippers. All the remaining four churches, and the Parish Church, had a combination of free and rented seats. Consequently, within the town not only were there not enough churches, but of those that did exist, the accommodation available to the poor was limited. A significant amount of this unsatisfied demand was provided by Nonconformity, although the latter's chapels invariably contained rented pews too. Nevertheless, when Hook arrived in Leeds, he quickly realised the challenge of Nonconformity. Indeed, in a letter of July 1837 to the Revd Samuel Wilberforce (later to become Bishop of Oxford), Hook wrote:

> As to Church feeling, to Catholicism, the thing is utterly unknown to clergy and laity. … The *de facto* established religion here is Methodism, and the best of our church people, I mean the most pious, talk the language of Methodism; the traditional religion is Methodism.[6]

Specifically, the Anglicans had to compete with 28 dissenting chapels, 18 of which belonged to the various divisions or factions of Methodism (Wesleyan, New Connexion, Primitive Protestant). Next came the Independent (six) and Baptist (two), and finally the chapels of 'Old Dissent' – Quaker and Unitarian (two). The Roman Catholics were represented by three chapels (St Mary's, St Patrick's and St Ann's). The seats per head of population in 1837 were: Protestant Dissent (32 per cent), Anglican (16.1 per cent), Roman Catholic (2.4 per cent).[7] Even more worrying for Hook was that in 1839, the *Leeds Mercury* estimated that, of the 60,000 persons of worshipping age, some 40,000 attended neither a church nor a chapel on Sundays.[8]

Leeds in 1837

The Parish Church itself was situated at the centre of the most insanitary and poverty-stricken district. Within a few hundred yards, on the northern side of Kirkgate, 'at the bottom of Boot and Shoe Yard a fetid water course commencing in Vicar Lane receives much of the soil (sewage) from St George's Street and Court and other places in the vicinity. … Families were crowded into single rooms, the worst being the part-below ground cellar dwellings'. Similar conditions applied to the Bank (Quarry Hill) area to the East in which Irish immigrants were concentrated. Such living conditions led to periodic outbreaks of Cholera from 1832.[9]

Leeds was indeed a town of 'Two Nations'. 'Until the localities of the abodes of the working classes are rendered more approachable to the higher classes of their fellow citizens by the removal of many disgusting objects of sight and smell which abound in every quarter it is in vain to expect that any useful intercourse can be maintained'. Throughout his vicariate, Dr Hook and his family resided at the vicarage in Park Place, on the more salubrious, although gradually declining, west side of town, but within easy reach of the centre. From his daily walk from vicarage to church, the disgrace of the 'Two Nations' must have been particularly evident to Hook and doubtless this lay at the heart of his social, as well as his religious zeal.[10]

Hook's strategy for church extension

The above gives an indication of Hook's new parish. A lesser individual might have been prepared to accept its enormous social problems as an inevitable product of rapid industrialization. However, the new vicar was not. Even while he was engaged in the mammoth task of rebuilding his decayed medieval parish church, he was also considering how best to extend worship provision elsewhere within his huge parish. However, as a manufacturing parish with insufficient church provision, Leeds was far from unique. An obvious solution across the nation was the creation of more parishes, but this apparently rational solution was beset with various legal problems, ones often so great that they were deemed insurmountable.[11] Far easier – although still not also without legal challenges – was the erection of chapels of ease, the solution usually adopted by those determined to build. It is paradoxical that – and as many friends of the Church of England complained – while the Nonconformists and Roman Catholics could build new places of worship wherever they wanted with only very few formalities to constrain them, the Church of England was severely hampered by its status as the Established Church, governed by Parliament.

However Hook, never a man to take the easy route where a more beneficial alternative was achievable, rejected the chapel of ease option. His argument was that his new churches should have their own vicar rather than a 'mere' chapel curate. Thus, soon after his arrival in Leeds, he began to formulate a scheme to divide the vast parish to create additional, smaller ones.[12] This really was an exceedingly ambitious strategy, one very rarely considered anywhere else in England in this period. The first episode in his plan came in 1839 with fund-raising for St Luke, North Street, 'to serve a poor and uninstructed population'. Money was raised in Leeds and also in Oxford through the endeavours of Hook's senior curate who still had connections in the city. And it was grant-aided by the Ripon Diocesan Church Building Society (RDCBS), founded in 1838 by Bishop Longley, first diocesan of the see of Ripon, established in 1836.[13] The foundation stone was laid by Dr Hook in 1839. It was a small church with just 426 sittings. This was followed by St Andrew, Cavendish Street, begun in 1842.

More dynamically, in 1843 Hook's plan began to assume a definite shape and in that year he wrote to his old friend, W. P. Wood,

> one thing I have determined on, I shall divide this living and sink from Vicar of Leeds to incumbent of St Peter's. I propose to constitute all the existing churches as parish churches and I will give up £400 out of my £1200 on condition that the Ecclesiastical Commissioners will purchase the pews [pew rents] of the churches and make them free.

To give up one third of his stipend really was selfless, as well as being almost unparalleled. 'I shall give up all, and shall do so with joy save when I think of the beautiful house we have builded to the glory of God, for the use not of the little poor district of St Peter's only, but that of all Leeds. Our services we will keep up, come what may.'[14]

Hook's scheme for the break-up of the Parish of Leeds took final form in January 1844 in an open letter to the parishioners of Leeds. In this long document, Hook proposed that

> both the existing churches [chapels of ease] in the out-townships and those yet to be built in the in-township of Leeds should become parishes with a resident incumbent with the sole cure of souls and full powers of vicars in immediate subordination to the Bishop [of Ripon] … no church to become a Parish Church until the floor [i.e. the nave] had been declared free and open to the inhabitants. … The advantages of a resident parochial clergyman in each parish and district will thus be secured and the church system fully restored … I am most anxious to secure for my poorer brethren the privileges of a free and unrestricted participation in the sacraments and ordinances of our holy church … and I hope soon to see Schools established in every parish by the liberality of the National Society … *We must never rest until we have provided for every poor man a pastor and every poor child a School.*[15]

Hook's patent generosity was widely applauded although it was greeted by alarm from Dissenters concerned at the prospect of chapels of ease being converted to parish churches and non-resident curates without cure of souls becoming resident vicars. The legal machinery by which Hook planned to execute these reforms had to be *via* an Act of Parliament – the Leeds Vicarage Act of 1844 – which cost some £1,400 in fees, even though unopposed, although it was subject to two significant modifications.[16]

In the event only a limited use was made of the provisions of the Leeds Vicarage Act. Except for the new parish of St Saviour – discussed

Fig. 5.2: St Andrew, Cavendish Street (George Gilbert Scott, 1842–5). (Leeds University Library, Special Collections)

Fig. 5.3: St Saviour, The Bank (J. M. Derick, 1841–5)

Fig. 5.4: St Philip, Wellington Street (R. D. Chantrell, 1845–7)

below – it was primarily used to confer parochial status to the out-township chapelries. Much greater use was made of Sir Robert Peel's *The Spiritual Care of Populous Parishes Act* of 1843, which provided both a resident clergyman and an endowment for his stipend. He would be appointed before his church was built so he could be involved in fundraising and the creation of his new parish.[17] Listed below are the eighteen churches erected 1837–59 during Hooks vicariate and consecrated by Bishop Longley. Map 5.2 shows the locations of fifteen of these churches within, or just beyond, the one-mile radius of Leeds Parish Church, including St George, begun just before Hook's arrival.

Churches erected in the parish of Leeds during Dr Hook's vicariate, 1837-59

(Architect, date of consecration and number of sittings in brackets)

- **St Thomas, Stanningley, 1839–41** (Henry Rogerson, 2 April, 500). Built as a result of the initiative of Thomas Furbank, incumbent of Bramley for 'the poor working population'. Funded by subscription and RDCBS grant.
- **St Peter (Leeds Parish Church) 1838–41** (R. D. Chantrell, 2 Sept, 2,400) [see Paper 2 by Christopher Webster].
- **St Luke, North Street, 1839–41** (Perkin & Backhouse, 4 October, 277). Cost: £1,300. Subscription-funded to serve a poor and populous district. Foundation stone laid by Hook, 1839. *Demolished 1937.*
- **St Andrew, Cavendish Street, 1842–45** (George Gilbert Scott, 26 March, 852) (Fig. 5.2). Built under Peel's Act, in memory of Mrs Helen Sinclair, wife of the first incumbent of St George. The project included a school. Recipient of RDCBS and Commissioners' grants. *Demolished 1960.*
- **St Saviour, The Bank, 1841–1845** (J. M. Derick, 28 October, 550) (Fig. 5.3). Founded (anonymously) and entirely funded by Dr E. B. Pusey in response to a letter of 1839 from Dr Hook 'of the need for a church in a populous and poor district'. Original dedication, the Church of the Holy Cross, changed to St Saviour's by Bishop Longley. Built under Hook's Leeds Vicarage Act.
- **St Philip, Wellington Street, 1845–47** (R. D. Chantrell, 7 October, 587) (Fig. 5.4). Funded by subscription and grants, and by mill-owner John Gott. *Demolished 1931.*
- **Holy Trinity, Meanwood, 1847–49** (William Railton, 6 October, 400) (Fig. 5.5). Built under Peel's Act. Founded by Mary and Elizabeth Beckett in memory of their brother, Christopher, and on land given by his brother, Sir John Beckett. It cost over £4,300 and accommodated 400.[18]

- **All Saints, York Road, 1847–50** (Philip Boyce, 1 November, 600). Parish founded under the terms of the Leeds Vicarage Act but Hook expedited the creation and endowment of a Peel District. Funded by subscription and RDCBS and Commissioners' grants. *Demolished 1980.* Replaced by a new church.
- **St John the Evangelist, Little Holbeck 1847–50** (George Gilbert Scott, 2 November, 700) (Fig 5.6). School and clergyman provided under the terms of Peel's Act. Built and endowed by J. G and H. C. Marshall (flax spinners). *Demolished 1938.*
- **St Matthew, Little London, 1846–51** (C. W. Burleigh, 13 August, 700) (Fig. 5.7). Parish established under Peel's Act. Cost £2,800 with 700 seats. Funded by subscription and RDCBS and Commissioners' grants.[19] *Demolished c.1965.*
- **St Thomas, Melbourne Street, The Leylands, 1850–52** (William Butterfield, 2 February, 800) (Fig. 5.8). Entirely paid for by M. J. Rhodes, a Leeds merchant. *Demolished c.1940.*
- **St Jude, Pottery Fields, 1852–53** (Philip Boyce, 26 October, 600). Gothic with NW tower. Parish established under Peel's Act. Funded by RDCBS and Commissioners' grants, plus a substantial donation. *Demolished c.1935.*
- **St John the Baptist, New Wortley 1852–53** (Dobson & Chorley, 17 November, 700) (Fig. 5.9). Parish established under Peel's Act. Funded by RDCBS and Commissioners' grants, plus a substantial donation. *Demolished 1957.*
- **St John the Evangelist, Moor Allerton 1845–53** (Joseph Thompson, 13 December, 250). Cost £1,106. Project led by John Urquhart, incumbent of Chapel Allerton. Funded by local gentry, subscriptions and a RDCBS grant of £200. 250 sittings, 150 free or let at small rental.
- **St Michael, Buslingthorpe 1852–54** (C. W. Burleigh, 17 April, 600). Parish established under Peel's Act. Funded by subscriptions, RDCBS and Commissioners' grants. *Demolished 1957.*
- **St Stephen, Burmantofts 1853–54** (Jeremiah Dobson, 9 November, 490) (Fig. 5.10). Parish established under Peel's Act. Funded by subscriptions, plus grants from RDCBS, ICBS and Commissioners. *Demolished 1938.*
- **St Matthias, Burley 1853–54** (Perkin & Backhouse, 11 November, 450). Estimated cost, £3,050. Parish constituted under Peel's Act. Funded by William Beckett, subscriptions and RDCBS grant (£375).
- **St Barnabas, Little Holbeck 1854–1855** (J. T. Fairbank, 5 December, 560). Parish constituted under Peel's Act. Site donated; funded by RDCBS and Commissioners' grants. *Demolished 1938.*

Fig. 5.5: Holy Trinity, Meanwood (William Railton, 1847–9). (Leeds University Library, Special Collections)

Fig. 5.6: St John the Evangelist, Little Holbeck (George Gilbert Scott, 1847–50). (Leeds University Library, Special Collections)

Fig. 5.7: St Matthew, Little London (C. W. Burleigh, 1846). (Leeds Library and Information Services)

Fig. 5.8: St Thomas, Melbourne Street (William Butterfield, 1850–2). (Leeds University Library, Special Collections)

Fig. 5.9: St John the Baptist, New Wortley (Dobson & Chorley, 1852–3). (Leeds University Library, Special Collections)

How was Hook's building programme financed?

An examination of this remarkable building programme naturally leads to the question: 'how did Hook raise the necessary finance?' We do not have precise costs for all eighteen of Hook's churches, but with an average cost of around £3,000, plus £30,000 for the new Parish Church, the bill was approximately £80,000,[20] which equates to over £8,000,000 at 2022 prices.

What is clear is that Hook had a range of funding sources which he could exploit: grants (discussed below); subscriptions could be sought from middle-class – but not necessarily very affluent – members of the new congregation who might be rewarded with a free pew for a number of years; and exceptionally wealthy elites might be courted to provide the site, the building or an endowment for the minister.[21] Aside from the Parish Church, some examples will be illuminating.

St Philip, Bean Ings, Wellington Street (1845–7), was situated on the western fringe of the in-township, an area with 'no fewer than 12,000 inhabitants,[22] occupied 'chiefly by the sons and daughters of toil', many employed at the huge mill opposite owned by the Gott family[23] (Fig. 5.4). The site was 'given by Messrs Gott' who also gave half the cost of its erection.[24] The rest came from 'subscriptions'. Both £3,371 and £5,231 are given as the final cost.[25] It accommodated 587 persons, only 144 of which were free.[26] One can assume the subscribers taking the rented pews came from the genteel streets just to the north of this district. A grant of £300 came from the Commissioners and one for £200 from the ICBS.[27] The Revd Sinclear, the incumbent at St George in whose district St Philip was situated, appears to have taken a lead in the project; interestingly, newspaper reports and correspondence rarely mention Hook. Also collections were made at the opening services – collections were generally taken only on special occasions, rather than at every service as today – in aid of the district's schools and to erect a master's house.[28]

St John the Evangelist, Little Holbeck (1847–50) was built by 'the munificence of James Garth Marshall Esq and the firm with which he is connected'[29] (Fig 5.6).'Funding also came from Henry Cowper Marshall, Esq., his brother.'[30] In addition, the Marshalls gave '£250 a year as an endowment, plus £500 in a 3% investment as a repair fund.'[31] 'Always conscious if his social responsibilities,' he and his family also paid for schools in Holbeck as well as allotments in Headingley.[32]

For St Stephen, Burmantofts (c.1853–4), the project was funded by a larger number of donors each giving more modest sums: William Beckett, MP, £200; John Gott, Esq, £100; John Atkinson, Esq, £100; J. P. Garlick, Esq, £100; Edw. Wilkinson, Esq, £100; Wm. Williams Brown, Esq, £50; Js. Brown Esq, £50; Revd F. T. Rowell, £50 plus a further £75;

J. Hardy, Esq, £50; and Wm Hey Esq, £25 (Fig. 5.10). In addition, there were 'grants [of £500] from the RDCBS and [£200 from] the Commissioners, [and the] proceedings of a bazaar'.[33] The architect's estimated cost was £2,685.[34] Thus grants and large donations covered well over half the cost of the building; the remainder came from smaller donations. The site was a gift from the Revd Rowell and J. Atkinson Esq, and a legacy from Mrs Matthewman produced £150 per annum as an endowment plus money for the repair fund. All the 605 seats were free.[35]

The site for St Barnabas, Holbeck (1854–5) was given by Thomas Benyon Esq, and Mrs Henry Benyon. The church was paid for by subscription and grants from the RDCBS, the Commissioners and the ICBS. It cost £3,000.[36]

Hook succeeded in securing some massive donations from individuals: £2,000 for St Jude, Pottery Field, and £1,000 for St John the

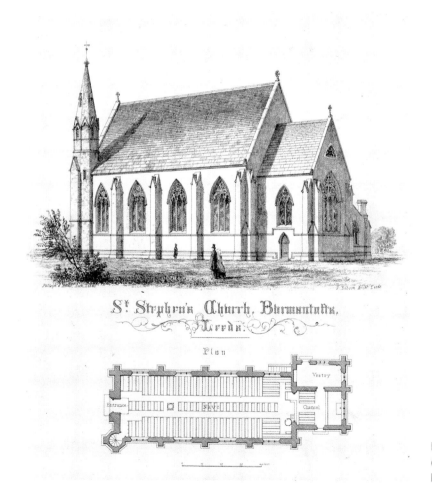

Fig. 5.10: St Stephen, Burmantofts (Jeremiah Dobson, 1853–4). (Leeds Library and Information Services)

Baptist, New Wortley. For All Saints, York Road, the *Mercury* reported 'Dr Hook has received a donation for £500 towards to the erection of [this] church [from an unnamed individual who was at the consecration of St Saviours].'[37] William Beckett, banker and MP was another generous donor for both churches and schools.[38] These huge gifts are indicative of what could be achieved; no doubt Hook was adept at courting donors. Indeed, the *Mercury* reported that for New Wortley, he secured funding only by 'begging most assiduously' (Fig. 5.9).[39] And for the 'attached' school, New Wortley's vicar and his curate dispatched 22,000 letters seeking funds (see Fig. 5.13).[40] However, apparently selfless generosity might not be without problems as the case of St Saviour's illustrates. This impressive church, erected at an eye-watering cost of £16,000, was the result of a gift from Oxford luminary, Dr Pusey, enthusiastic to extend the reach of Tractarianism by provocatively founding a church in hitherto middle-of-the-road Leeds where he could, not unreasonably, dictated the liturgy that was to take place in 'his' church; its Anglo-Catholicism did not please Hook, nor the bishop, as noted below.[41]

Grants

There were a number of grant-giving bodies that could be approached, principally the Commissions, the ICBS – both based in London – and the local Ripon Diocesan Church Building Society (RDCBS). Several Hook churches were funded by grants in addition to donations. For St Michael, Buslingthorpe, 'the site has been presented by Benjamin Wainman, Esq. [The church] cost £1,700 which has been raised by public subscription, assisted by grants from the Commissioners and the Ripon Diocesan Society.'[42] Indeed, nine Hook churches received Commissioners' funding with sums varying from £250–£350, typically, £300; most cost around £3,000.[43] St John the Baptist, New Wortley, was the most expensive at £3,457 (Fig. 5.9), and St Barnabas, Little Holbeck, the cheapest at £1,660.[44]

Several churches, including St Barnabas, Little Holbeck and St Andrew, Cavendish Street (Fig. 5.3), were the recipients of ICBS grants.[45] More significant was the RDCBS, founded in 1838; with Leeds the largest town in the diocese, it is not surprising it was generous. In just one year, 1849, the following grants were awarded to Hook's projects: £375 for the new church at Burley; £200 for the new Church at Moor Allerton. Plans for St Thomas, Leylands (Fig 5.8), and All Saints, York Road, were approved with grants to follow. There was also a grant of £200 for new clergy houses at Armley, Burley, Moor-Allerton and St Luke, Leeds.[46]

Hook's attitude to pew-renting

Like many clerics of his generation, Hook was committed to the notion that all were equal in the sight of God.[47] In this context, he not unreasonably objected to rented pews, although he recognised their necessity to cover on-going costs. Part of Hook's fund-raising ambition involved the collection of sufficient funds to provide investments – usually 3 per cent bonds – where the interest would take care of these bills. Thus many of Hook's new churches had no rented seats, a most unusual occurrence in the mid-century. By way of example, of 322 churches erected across England between 1840 and 1856 which were the recipients of Commissioners' grants, just 57 had no rented pews; 5 of them were in Leeds.[48] These were: All Saints, York Road; St John the Baptist, New Wortley; St Jude, Hunslet (Pottery Field); St Michael Buslingthorpe; St Stephen, Burmantofts.

Contemporary notices of Hook's Leeds churches in *The Ecclesiologist* and *The Builder*

Five of the 'Hook churches' were described by *The Ecclesiologist* in articlers written in the first person plural and in prose both lofty and condescending. Of St Philip, Wellington Street, it noted that 'while somewhat plain and commonplace, we ought to be thankful for a church as good as this in a manufacturing town' (Fig. 5.4).[49] For St Matthew, Little London, it recorded 'we have examined with great pleasure the designs' (Fig. 5.7).[50] St Jude, Pottery Fields, designed by Philip Boyce, a member of the society, 'is a decided success'.[51] However, the greatest praise is accorded to Butterfield's St Thomas, Melbourne Street (Fig. 5.8): 'After the miserable structures which vex an Ecclesiologist wherever he may be; in Leeds it is a comfort to come across a building which, in spite of its faults, and in its faults, shows the hand of a master … but it is the whole effect and not the details by which this church is to be judged and so considered is quite worthy of the architect of All Saints, Margaret Street.'[52]. Of Holy Trinity, Meanwood (Fig. 5.5), discussed in a long article, it was less enthusiastic. 'It is not what might have been expected in the present day. It does not (to our mind) at all realise the idea of a village church.'[53] St Saviour is addressed below.

Of these five, only Holy Trinity, Meanwood, and St Saviour, are still standing. In 1847, the latter was described in in prose which reached new heights. 'Who that has watched the church movement in England can be ignorant of the history of St Saviour, Leeds, of the deep anonymous piety that led to its foundation, of the revered name which presided over its rising walls, the cloud which seemed for a while to rest upon it, of the bright sunshine which succeeded.'[54] The writer, clearly from Cambridge, is not unaware of the poverty and destitution of this area of Leeds.

> We fancied as we suppose is the case with most of our readers who have not seen it that the church was immured in some collection of frightful and fetid alleys: we were accordingly not a little surprised at the real beauty and grandeur of its situation. It stands on a high and rather steep hill somewhat on the outskirts of the town with a wide prospect. As we mount the steep bank … the structure, now seen obliquely, greatly improves upon us, developing its form and grouping with the college (the clergy house) … the style is middle-pointed and it is hoped in time to crown the church with a lofty tower and spire… the first aspect when we enter St Saviour's is extremely impressive and religious.

After a detailed description of the painted glass and fittings of the church the writer concludes 'we see a wonderful improvement over St Peter's (the Parish Church) which can now be regarded as an historical monument.'[55]

St Saviour is a church of national importance (Figs 3.5, 5.3). Funded anonymously by E. B. Pusey, it was the first church to be built in which the objectives of the Oxford Tractarian movement were to be realized at parish level. But the high hopes at its foundation soon disintegrated under accusations of popery in its liturgy and practices, and the defection of some members of its clergy and parishioners to Rome – the 'cloud' alluded to in *The Ecclesiologist*. Worse, it brought about a nearly complete rupture in the long friendship between Hook and Pusey.[56] Hook's concern was that St Saviour could undo all the pastoral successes which he had achieved in Leeds, a town, like so many others, where, at this time, there was real hatred of anything suggestive of popery. Both were adamant. In 1846 Pusey wrote to Hook, 'You talk about fighting popery – I really do not know what you are talking about. St Saviour's by your Act [Leeds Vicarage Act] is a distinct cure. You are no more responsible for St Saviour's than London'. Hook replied 'Be it so, but if my neighbour has a hornets nest and my children are likely to be stung I must ask him to remove it or I shall send to the constable (see Fig. 3.6).[57] Today, popery has lost its sting. St Saviour and its daughter church, St Hilda, continue the Anglo-Catholic tradition in Leeds.

In May 1852 members of the Yorkshire Architectural Society visited two recently completed churches – St John the Evangelist in Holbeck and St Thomas in the Leylands. Their observations and comments were recorded in *Reports and Papers of Architectural Societies*. All their praise was reserved for St John's which 'presents perhaps one of the most complete and costly structures which has been erected since the revival'. Nothing is said of St Thomas – praised by *The Ecclesiologist*, as noted above – except that 'Mr Butterfield's brick church of St Thomas was also visited'.[58] Clearly, St John and St Thomas, by any criterion, were outstanding churches. But here, in the report of the Society's visit in the *The Builder*, we encounter a rare indication of Hook's architectural philosophy.

> *Yorkshire Society* – last week this society examined St John's Church and St Thomas' Church, in Leeds, both of which have been lately erected, and examined the architectural designs of both edifices. At a meeting afterwards, the Rev. Dr. Hook, on taking the chair, remarked that if, at any time, an architectural society were a valuable institution, it is especially so in an age like our own, which has, to its disgrace, no style of its own. The future historian will have to record that there exists, so far as the church is concerned, no architectural style of the nineteenth century. We have been building churches for the last half-century, but instead of considering our requirements, and building churches adapted to the liturgy of the nineteenth century, we have been servile imitators of the churches of the fourteenth century. Our successors will hold us in derision when they record that to meet the wants of the reformed liturgy we built churches on the model of those erected to meet the wants of the unreformed [Catholic] liturgy. It is time we began to act on sounder principles. The examination of the ancient churches is important, for all new principles to be correct must be based on old principles; modern civilisation is closely connected with ancient civilisation and historical investigation and antiquarian research are necessary as well as independence of thought. Still the time he hoped was to come, or was coming, when architects would refuse to become mere imitators, and would give full play to their genius and their powers of invention in adapting buildings to our existing wants.[59]

In making these apparently radical assertions that 'reformed' Anglicanism needed a style of its own, not 'servile imitation' of a past one, Hook was essentially rehearsing opinions held by a broad range of commentators from the beginning of the century.[60] However, with this issue kept absolutely beyond discussion by the Ecclesiologists, and ardent advocates like Butterfield, it was a brave man that would question the suitability of medieval Gothic and internal plans developed for Roman Catholic worship, for the new Protestant churches. We are left with the clear impression, also evident in the accompanying paper by Dr Webster, that Hook combined a deep Toryism with an equally deep radicalism. So far as his attitude to modern ecclesiastical architecture is concerned, it would be reasonable to conclude that Hook differentiated between style and layout: he was enthusistic to promote Gothic for the new churches; what he objected to was the use of pre-Reformation plans for the reformed liturgy, especially deep, narrow chancels. Probably, the new St Saviour served to reinforce this opinion.

Hook's school-building programme: 'For every poor child a school'

Hook was also dynamic as a school-builder (Figs 5.11–5.15). And he established 'the Anglican Board of Education for Leeds which in turn saw the provision of twenty-seven new church schools'.[61]

Until the early years of the nineteenth century there was no system of national education – the grammar and charity Schools could only provide for a small number of children. Apart from learning the stories in the Bible and the alphabet, most children (particularly those from the poorest families) received no education at all. The situation changed significantly in the first decade of the century as a result of the foundation of the two societies: the overtly Anglican *The National Society for Promoting the Education of the Poor in the Principles of the Established Church*, founded by Andrew Bell, an Anglican clergyman, and the non-denominational Royal Lancastrian Society, established by Joseph Lancaster, a Quaker, and afterwards called *The British and Foreign Schools Society*. Both relied for their income on voluntary contributions and both operated the monitorial system. In this arrangement the older children (who had acquired some skills in reading and writing – i.e. the monitors) – taught, in turn, the younger children. Provision was cheap and the privilege of being a monitor and of being in a position of authority and influence in the school helped to maintain discipline. However, the quality of teaching was not only highly variable but was not subject to any kind of rigorous assessment. The monitorial system in both societies was largely superseded by trained teachers from about 1847. Dr Hook was, of course, a supporter of the National Society and established National Schools in the newly-formed parishes in Leeds, sometimes in advance of church itself (e.g. at St Saviour's, The Bank (Fig. 5.12) and Holy Trinity, Meanwood). However, he began to doubt that a voluntary system of education could ever reach the great mass of children. He realised that if they were to be educated (at National Schools) in Church principles, the schools needed greater funding than local sources could be relied on to provide. In a letter of July 1843 to Samuel Wilberforce (then Archdeacon of Westminster) he wrote:

I would not have the State take away the funds of the church, but I would have the Church make an offer of them. We want not proud Lords, haughty spiritual Peers, to be our Bishops. Offer four thousand out of their five thousand a year for the education of the people, and call upon the more wealthy of the other clergy to do the same and a fund at once is provided. Let Farnham Castle and Winchester House and Ripon Palace [all bishops' palaces] be sold, and we shall have funds to establish other Bishoprics. Let the Church do something like this and *then* the Church will live in the hearts of the people who now detest her.[62]

Wilberforce could not agree. His view (at that time, although modified in later life) was that such a course as Hook proposed 'would only be the hopeless career of revolution. There has been, I suppose, always poverty, always want, yet God has ordained differences of rank and intended his Church to pervade all ranks'.[63] It was not a reply to which Hook could readily acquiesce. In 1846, following a fact-finding correspondence with Mr Kay-Shuttleworth, secretary to the Education Committee of the Privy Council, he published an open letter (addressed as was the custom in those days) to a prominent person – in this case Bishop Thirlwall of St David's entitled: *How to rend more efficient the Education of the People.*

Hook pulled no punches. While expressing his admiration for all that the religious bodies had done he called their efforts 'Lighting a

Fig. 5.11: Christ Church School, Meadow Lane, Leeds (R. D. Chantrell, 1839–42). (Leeds Library and Information Services)

candle which only makes us more sensible of the surrounding darkness'. With no authority to enforce compulsory attendance they were faced with an impossible task. He now realized that 'only the state had the resources to establish and finance Schools, provide trained teachers and impose compulsory attendance – the money to be raised from a County rate and administered by Boards of Managers'.[64]

Hook never contended that his plan was perfect, but claimed that it was the only possible one for the time. He was indifferent alike to praise and blame. 'I know' he said, 'I am right and when it is too late churchmen will see that I am right'.[65] Nearly 100 years later, in the Education Act of 1944, provision was made for something like the type of school he would have wanted.

Education was not the only revolutionary measure that Hook supported; we have already noticed his radical views on church architecture. In addition, he was in favour of Jews and Roman Catholics sitting in Parliament; he attacked the evils of the factory system and supported the 10 Hours Bill; he urged that the bishops should leave the House of Lords and that their salaries be reduced. Hook's greatness as a parish priest has been fully recognised but the breadth and fertility of his ideas on educational, social, architectural and ecclesiastical reform have yet to receive the notice they deserve.

Fig. 5.12: The Bank National School (R. D. Chantrell, c.1840). (Christopher Webster)

Fig. 5.13 New Wortley National School (C. W. Burleigh, 1845). (Leeds Library and Information Services)

Hook's church building legacy

As shown above, twelve of the eighteen churches built during Hook's vicariate have been demolished and as shown in Map 5.2 all of these (indicated by red dots) lie within, or just outside, the 1-mile radius from the Parish Church. Within this area only St Saviour's (and the Parish Church itself), are extant (indicated by green dots).

Did Hook build his churches in the wrong places? While we can regret the loss of so many fine churches, this was, surely, an inevitable consequence of the shift of population from the inner-city area to the distant suburbs, together with the rise of Irish immigration, particularly in the Quarry Hill area from the 1850s, and that of Jewish immigration in the Leylands area from the 1870s. And ambitious, twentieth-century inner-city road schemes have entirely removed whole communities. Furthermore, it must be acknowledged that many of the sites for Hook's churches were given by the wealthy individuals who owned the land; in some cases – for instance, St Philip, Wellington Street and Holy Trinity, Meanwood – these individuals also contributed generously to building costs. Perhaps Hook was content to let these benefactors dictate locations. And might a smaller number of bigger churches – each more generously staffed by a vicar and a team of curates – have fared better? Certainly this was the opinion of architect J. T. Micklethwaite, one cogently promoted in his 1874 publication.[66]

Not only are the majority of Hook's churches no longer extant, they have been very poorly recorded photographically or not at all. There are no photographs of St John's and St Barnabas' churches prior to their demolition in 1938 when the parishes were amalgamated and worship was relocated to the council estate of Belle Isle. St John's, a considerable work of G. G. Scott, is a particularly grievous loss. H. S. Goodhart-Rendel recalls 'When the vaulted choir of the beautiful Temple Church in London had met its doom in the last war, I felt it consoling to reflect that Sir Gilbert Scott's miniature copy of it in the slums of Leeds would display the beauty of its form to future generations. When, the other day, I hunted for it, map in hand, it was gone; effaced not, I was told, by enemy action, but by its guardians, who had no further use for it.'[67]

Butterfield's church of St Thomas in the Leylands is perhaps an even greater loss and has a longer and more protracted history of decline, renewal and decline. Its founder, M. J. Rhodes, a wealthy cloth merchant and landowner and, like Butterfield, a member of the Margaret Chapel Fraternity, paid for the whole cost of the church erected on land that had been in the family's possession since 1792. Rhodes defected to the Roman Catholic Church before the building was completed and this

Fig. 5.14: Burley National School (Perkin & Backhouse, C. W. Burleigh, 1846). (Leeds Library and Information Services)

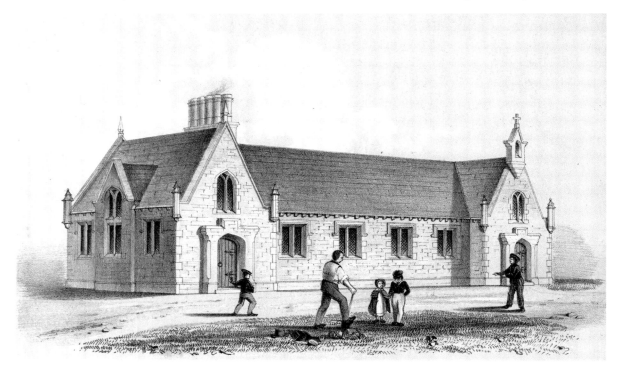

Fig. 5.15: St Peter's Parish Church School (Dobson & Chorley, c.1856–7).
(*The Builder*, 14, 1856, 663)

may well be the reason why he failed to pay for the proposed altar piece commissioned from Overbeck – Butterfield subsequently arranged for its sale to Beresford Hope. As early as 1855 decline set in although attempts were made to recover with special services in Hebrew. Given the rising Jewish population and increasing overcrowding and insanitary conditions in the courts and terraces of the Leylands the building of the chancel in 1891–3 – a last work of Butterfield – was a remarkable act of optimism that the church could flourish in such circumstances.

The report of the commission appointed by the Bishop of Ripon in 1900 proposed that the parishes of St Luke's and St Thomas' should be united and that St Thomas' church (which the commission recognized as 'a very fine one') should become the Parish Church. But decline continued and in the 1929 report of another commission, it was recommended that 'the Churches of St Thomas and St Luke be pulled down and the sites sold'.[68]

There remain five Anglican churches in the centre of Leeds: St John's, New Briggate, now in the care of the Churches Conservation Trust; Holy Trinity, Boar Lane (recently reordered as a 'midweek, city-centre worship hub'); St George's (Evangelical); St Saviour's (Anglo-Catholic) and St Peter's Parish Church (now Leeds Minster). These last three churches may be taken as representative of the whole spectrum of Anglican churchmanship: 'there's High Church, Low Church and Leeds Parish Church'.[69]

Conclusions

In the twenty-two years Hook was in Leeds, not only did his ministry transform the town's commitment to the Church of England, but, remarkably, he was a dynamic fund-raiser and builder. According to Rusby, 'Hook found the parish of Leeds with fifteen churches and left it with thirty-six; he found it with three schools and left it with thirty; he found it with six parsonage-houses and left it with twenty-nine'.[70] It was a staggering achievement. Just a year after arriving in the town, he played a significant role in the establishment of the Ripon Diocesan Church Building Society. In 1857 he was instrumental in establishing the Leeds Church Institute as a means of promoting Anglicanism in the town *via* its library, meeting rooms and a place of learning for young people. It was the home of a host of Church organisations and it remains active, although now ecumenical. After he had left Leeds, his ambitious plans were continued by the Leeds Church Extension Society, established in 1864. As a result of Hook's energy and ambition, Leeds came to be seen as 'the model parish of England', even in the United States[71] and, not unreasonably, Hook himself as 'the greatest parish priest of the [nineteenth] century'.[72] He had put new heart into those that remained faithful to the Church prior to his arrival and recruited new congregants in huge numbers by making it attractive and relevant to the whole community, rich and poor. Services at the Parish Church regularly attracted worshippers counted in thousands.[73] His was a truly remarkable achievement.

Notes

1. W. R. W. Stephens, *The Life and Times of Walter Farquhar Hook* 2 vols (London, 1879), 1, 369.
2. Erected 1794 as a Nonconformist chapel, bought by Anglican the Revd John King and consecrated 1801.
3. Erected *c*.1780, intended to be an Anglican chapel, but initially let to a Nonconformist congregation. It was consecrated in 1813. R.V. Taylor, *Ecclesiastiae Leodienes* (Leeds, 1875), 511.
4. C. J. Morgan, 'Demographic Change, 1771–1911, Table 3' in D. Fraser (ed.), A *History of Modern Leeds* (Manchester, 1980), 52.
5. H. W. Dalton, 'Anglican Resurgence under W. F. Hook', (*PTS*, Leeds, 2002), 10.
6. Stephens, *Hook*, 1, 404.
7. H. W. Dalton, 'Walter Farquhar Hook', *PTS*, Leeds, 1990, 32.
8. *Leeds Mercury*, 29 December 1839.
9. Maurice Beresford, 'East End-West End' (*PTS*, Leeds, 1985–6), p. 392. See also *Leeds Intelligencer*, 30 September 1837; 17 July 1841.
10. Beresford, *East End-West End*, 383.

11. For more on this subject, see Christopher Webster, 'Late-Georgian Church-building: the legal and administrative challenges' in *Ecclesiology Today*, 61, 2022, forthcoming.

12. Stephens, *Hook*, 2, 166–73.

13. For the foundation of the society, see 'Register of Ecclesiastical Intelligence', 29–30 in *Church of England Magazine*, V, 1838.

14. Stephens, *Hook*, 2, 165. See also *Leeds Intelligencer*, 20 January 1844.

15. Stephens, *Hook*, 2, 166–73. The details of the Act are reproduced in *Leeds Intelligencer*, 22 June 1844.

16. For more detail of the Act, see H.W. Dalton, *Anglican Resurgence*, 101–2.

17. See Robert E. Rodes, *Law and Modernisation in the Church of England* (Notre Dame and London, 1991), 168.

18. *The Ecclesiologist*, X (N.S. VII), 1850, 237–40.

19. *The Ecclesiologist*, X (N.S. VII), 1850, 434.

20. An 1847 article about the new St Philip, Wellington Street, states that by then £30,000 had been raised for Hook's new churches, although it does not list the churches included in this calculation. *Leeds Intelligencer*, 9 October 1847.

21. More examples can be found in R.V. Taylor, *Ecclesiae Leodienses* (London, 1875).

22. *Leeds Intelligencer*, 9 October 1847.

23. Anon., *Historical Guide to Leeds* (Leeds, 1858), 61.

24. *Leeds Intelligencer*, 11 January 1845; 9 October 1847.

25. CBC, file 20547. However, Chantrell gave the cost as 'upwards of £5,000'. *The Builder*, 5, 1847, 508.

26. Michael Port, *600 New Churches* (Reading, 2006), 344

27. ICBS, file 03601.

28. *Leeds Mercury*, 2 October 1847.

29. *Leeds Mercury*, 13 November 1847.

30. Taylor, *Ecclesiae Leodienses*, 381.

31. Taylor, *Ecclesiae Leodienses*, 382.

32. David Thornton, *Leeds a Biographical Dictionary* (Leeds 2021), 194.

33. Taylor, *Ecclesiae Leodienses*, 238–9.

34. Port, *600 New Churches*, 344.

35. Taylor, *Ecclesiae Leodienses*, 239–40.

36. Taylor, *Ecclesiae Leodienses*, 386.

37. *Leeds Mercury*, 16 January 1847.

38. *Leeds intelligencer*, 3 April 1847.

39. *Leeds Mercury*, 26 November 1847.

40. *Leeds Mercury*, 18 November 1848.

41. Stephens, *Hook*, 2, 190–99. Dalton, *Hook*, 66–8.

42. Taylor, *Ecclesiae Leodienses*, 143. Port, 344, gives the cost as £2,170.

43. Port, *600 New Churches*, 344.

44. Port, *600 New Churches*, 344. Both these figures are architects' estimates; actual costs were likely to have been greater.

45. ICBS, files 04588 and 03317.

46. *Leeds Mercury*, 10 November 1849.

47. It is a theme to be found in numerous letters to journals in the period. For instance, *Gentleman's Magazine*, 1800, pt 2, 821–2.

48. Statistics compiled from Port, *600 New Churches*, 326–47.

49. *The Ecclesiologist*, VIII (N.S. V), 1847–8, 109–10.

50. *The Ecclesiologist*, X (N.S. VII), 1850, 434.

51. *The Ecclesiologist*, XV (N.S. XII), 1854, 60.

52. *The Ecclesiologist*, XV (N.S. XII), 1854, 59–60.

53. *The Ecclesiologist*, X (N.S. VII), 1850, 237–40.

54. *The Ecclesiologist*, VIII (N.S. V), 1847–8, 129–134.

55. *The Ecclesiologist*, VIII (N.S. V), 1847–8, 129–134.

56. Their long friendship began during undergraduate days at Oxford and was cemented by their mutual support for the Tractarian Movement. It was only two years before Hook's death that their cordial relationship was restored. Stephens, *Hook*, (1880 edition), 593–4. This correspondence does not appear in the 1879 edition.

57. H. P. Liddon, *Life of Edward Bouverie Pusey*, 3 vols (London, 1894), 3, 121, 125. Pusey to Hook, 14 November 1846; Hook to Pusey, 18 November 1846. *See* Roy Yates, 'St Saviour's Church, Leeds, and the Oxford Movement' in *Thoresby Society Miscellany*, 19, 2009, 1–36.

58. *Reports and Papers of Architectural Societies*, II, 1852–3, xviii.

59. *The Builder*, 10, 1852, 363.

60. For instance, E. J. Willson's 'Introduction' in Augustus Pugin, *Specimens of Gothic Architecture* (London, 1821), p. xix-xx; *Quarterly Review*, XXVII, 1822, 321; G. E. Street, 'The True Principles of Architecture and the Possibility of Development', lecture, reprinted in *The Ecclesiologist*, 13 (N.S. 10), 1852, 247– 62.

61. Thornton, *Leeds*, 136. However, an 1847 correspondent with the *Leeds Mercury* claimed there was already a problem in filling the school places that existed. *Leeds Mercury*, 9 January 1847.

62. C. J. Stranks, *Dean Hook*, (London, 1954), 74–5.

63. Stranks, *Hook*, 76.

64. Stranks, *Hook*, 78.

65. Stranks, *Hook*, 80.

66. J. T. Micklethwaite, *Modern Parish Churches* (London, 1874), 330–43.

67. H. S. Goodhart-Rendel, *Journal of the London Society*, 334, 1958, 8.

68. Parish records cease after 1936 but there is some uncertainty as to the dates of demolition of both churches. The *Bradford Observer* of 26 July 1938 states 'in Leeds downtown churches of one denomination or another are still being bowled over like proverbial ninepins and the latest to be demolished is St Thomas', Melbourne Street, a sister church of St Luke's which quite recently was razed to the ground'. However, there exists a photograph of St Luke, apparently taken by John Summerson in 1941–44 when he worked for the National Buildings Record and made extensive tours focusing on threatened or bomb damaged buildings.

69. The saying is sometimes attributed to John Betjeman, in a television broadcast *c*.1970, but almost certainly existed earlier.

70. Rusby, *Leeds Parish Church*, 69.

71. Thornton, *Biographical Dictionary*, 136.

72. Rusby, *Leeds Parish Church*, 66.

73. Dalton, 'Hook', 79.

6.

'... a Good Service ...': the Musical Tradition of Leeds Parish Church

SIMON LINDLEY and ALEXANDER WOODROW

When this paper was presented on 11 September 2021, seven musical excerpts were played during its course by the Minster's Sub-Organist, David Houlder. These were as follows:

1. Andante in E minor – S. S. Wesley
   (bar 82 to the end)
2. Cast me not away from thy presence – S. S. Wesley
   (choral parts realised on the organ, from 'make me to hear of joy and gladness' to the end)
3. Evening Song – E. C. Bairstow
   (final section of the ternary form structure, i.e. the final three pages)
4. Gloria of 'Communion Service in D' – E. C. Bairstow
   (four-bar organ introduction to the Gloria, preceding the first choral entry)
5. Hymn-Anthem: 'St Patrick's Breastplate' – Melville Cook
   (final 'descant' verse, with the organ and choral parts co-realised on the organ)
6. Hymnus Paschalis – Donald Hunt
   (final movement, with the organ and choral parts co-realised on the organ)
7. Choral Song – S. S. Wesley

'A good choir must be formed, [even] if I go to prison for it … My whole heart is set on this business.'[1] These are the words of Dr Hook, Vicar of Leeds between 1837 and 1859, the man responsible for the rebuilding of this church in 1841, as well as for the establishment of a daily choral service here, a regime that, most unusually for a parish church, continued well into the present century. Hook's fervent views on church music drove a programme of initiatives that laid the musical foundation of the church for the better part of the succeeding 200 years.[2] This paper seeks to examine Vicar Hook's visionary input and that of his first organist, Samuel Sebastian Wesley, along with their successors.

To take us back to the time of Hook and S. S. Wesley, let us first hear a brief section of Wesley's *Andante* in E minor; a poignant utterance of great expressive beauty, the harmonic structure of which bears a close affinity with a fine early anthem of Wesley's – *To my request and earnest cry*.[3] Wesley was no mean self-publicist and, as the foremost church musician of his day, his music was eagerly devoured, much of it privately printed and disseminated to his friends and colleagues as well as to the nation's choral foundations in a marketing exercise not dissimilar to the twentieth century 'demo tape' often deployed for the same purpose by popular musicians and their agents.

[Excerpt 1]

Arrangements for the period around the building of the new Parish Church included a series of lectures by Prebendary John Jebb of Limerick, widely acknowledged as the leading expert of the day in terms of choral services.[4] Jebb seems to have been entirely at variance with other contemporary leaders, such as Frederick Oakley, minister of the Margaret Street Chapel, London.[5] Despite the honoured historical place that the chapel's successor, All Saints' Margaret Street, holds in the history of the Church of England, it is perhaps worth pointing out that, following the Leeds consecration in 1841 – which was attended by such national figures as Dr Edward Pusey and Florence Nightingale – fully a further eighteen years were to elapse before the opening of the famous 'model' church in London's West End, with its clergy house and choir school surrounding the church's external courtyard. Oakley and his first organist, Richard Redhead, were entirely committed to unison chanting by means of Gregorian tones, rather than following the English tradition of Anglican chants first forthcoming from around the late seventeenth century.

What emerged from Jebb's lectures was not mere general interest, but rather a practical offer of assistance by volunteer men in singing with the choir of boys and men at the Sunday services in Leeds. As recently as the 1980s and 1990s, the definitions *Daily* and *Sunday* Choir were in widespread use, reflecting the distinction between a more extensive choir at weekends and festivals, with somewhat more modest weekday provision, for which the additional corpus of adult singers present usually only at weekends can be drawn upon as the basis of what is general known as a 'deputy list'. Hook proved himself more than adaptable to, and keen on, such a suggestion, which we believe was an entirely new procedure within an Anglican choral establishment, though nowadays extremely widespread in many foundations in 'quires and places where they sing'. This nineteenth-century Leeds pattern has proved itself splendidly within the cathedral tradition in Britain.

Study of the book containing the full details of the opening services in 1841 yields a number of points of interest, not least among them being what we might regard today as the rather four-square nature of the choral music involved – especially of the service music such as Canticles at Matins and Evensong as well as what was then known as the *Office of Holy Communion*.[6]

Samuel Sebastian Wesley, the most celebrated church musician of his day, had come to Leeds from his first cathedral appointments at Hereford and Exeter, and moved onto the cathedrals of Winchester and Gloucester in turn. As the first organist of the new Parish Church in Leeds Wesley [who had acted in that capacity for the consecration in 1841 and moved to Leeds the following year], wasted no time in publishing an edition of *Preces*, *Versicles* and *Responses* for use at Matins and Evensong. Whilst here in Leeds, Wesley completed a whole 'Service' in E major in 1845, from which still today the *Magnificat* and *Nunc Dimittis* (1843–4) are widely heard, with an occasional, much rarer, outing given to the first two components, the *Te Deum* and *Jubilate Deo*; although fine new editions by Peter Horton have been issued on behalf of the Church Music Society.

A further noble contribution to the Anglican choral repertoire, written in 1848 – the year before he left Yorkshire for Hampshire – is the extraordinary anthem *Cast me not away from Thy presence*. Not only is *Cast me not away* an exceptionally beautiful miniature, its deeply felt style harks back to a much earlier period in Anglican church music. Romantic as the expression may be said to be, the roots of the work are to be found within the older Renaissance tradition of unaccompanied polyphonic singing – often referred to as the 'golden age' of English music. A few famous chromatic bars right at the close inform us of the composer's serious injury to a leg, resulting in an extensive period of convalescence at the Black Swan in Helmsley; the pain of the injury is vividly expressed in the music that sets the words – somewhat ironically – 'that the bones that thou hast broken may rejoice!'

[Excerpt 2]

Leeds was widely acknowledged as possessing a very strong Nonconformist community at the outset of the nineteenth century. By the time Hook left for the Deanery of Chichester in 1859, he had created a vast Anglican infrastructure of additional churches, schools and parsonages across the once vast parish of Leeds, as set out in Christopher Hammond's paper. So far as the dramatic revival of attendance at the

Parish Church was concerned, the dignity of the services, and especially the quality of the music, were central. Indeed, in 1842, Hook told Pusey that, 'no cathedral in England could match the services at Leeds Parish Church for solemnity and grandeur'.[7] And although Wesley departed ten years before Hook, the great musical tradition they established continued. It is likely that Wesley's decision to leave Leeds and move to Winchester Cathedral was almost entirely determined by the opportunity on offer from Winchester College for the education of his five sons – only one of the offspring of Wesley and his wife was a daughter.

It is worth stating that the credit for the foundation of the Parish Church's choral tradition here in Leeds is often, and mistakenly, given exclusively to Dr Hook. That distinction properly belongs to an earlier nineteenth-century Vicar of Leeds, Richard Fawcett, incumbent here from 1815 for 22 years, who was succeeded after his death in 1837 by Hook, who had come from Holy Trinity, Coventry. Fawcett had arranged, probably as early as 1818, for the organisation of a paid choir of boys and men, costing £90 per year, financed by a charge on the Church Rate. It was placed within the 'old church', facing west, at the east end of the nave, adjacent to the organ that then stood on a handsome gallery.

Remarkably, it seems the choristers were robed, probably the first instance of this on the English mainland in a parish church since the Reformation. Positive proof of the robes seems to date from 1818 with the survival of a receipt for laundering the surplices for the boys[8] and certainly various articles in local newspapers confirm the existence of the robed choir comprising six men and six boys, in the mid-1820s.[9] However, in this strongly Nonconformist town, there was much opposition from the ratepayers who objected to funding these 'popish exhibitions'. At a noisy vestry meeting in 1826, one parishioner was heard to say that 'in his estimation, the idea of having a dozen persons dressed in surplices chaunting the praises of God … was not only a relic of popery; it was the dregs of popery'.[10] However, the motion was defeated, but a similar one in 1827 was successful.[11] The choir continued, funded by the congregation, rather than the rate payers, but around 1830, the surplices were discarded, to be found 'in rags' when Dr Hook arrived in 1837.[12] Nevertheless, in 1841, Hook revived the tradition of a robed choir for his new church. The weekday choir received remuneration, but the Sunday choir was comprised of volunteers.

It is said that 'what Wesley did for the organ' his erstwhile assistant and successor, Dewsbury-born Robert Senior Burton 'did for the choir'.[13] Burton, like his eventual twentieth-century successor, Donald Hunt, was tremendously active as a choral trainer throughout the North of England, being founder-conductor of the Leeds Music Festival of

1858 and of the Huddersfield Choral Society in addition to many other adult choral groups.[14] Upon retirement from the Parish Church in 1880, Burton moved to become Organist of St Peter's church in Harrogate, some twenty miles to the north.

Burton was succeeded in Leeds by William Creser who came from Scarborough and left Leeds to become organist of H.M. Chapels Royal in London. Records from this period include a good number of annual 'Combination Books' kept with candour as well as accuracy by successive holders of the office of precentor.

Following Creser's move to London in 1891, his place was taken in that year by Alfred Benton, who had held the office of organist and choirmaster at the parish of St Martin, Potternewton, in a genteel northern suburb of Leeds.

The first appointment of the twentieth century was undoubtedly the most significant since that of Wesley well over sixty years earlier. A native of Huddersfield, Edward Cuthbert Bairstow's earliest experience had been grounded in London, where he was an articled pupil to the legendary Sir Frederick Bridge at Westminster Abbey. He then furthered his skills at Wigan Parish Church in Lancashire in a four-year tenure from 1902, before moving to Leeds in 1906.[15]

Bairstow's 'Evening Song' of 1899 began life as a solo for cello with piano accompaniment but is now best known in his own version for solo organ. The melody begins life in the tenor register. It is said to have been Lady Bairstow's favourite of her husband's works and was apparently requested every year on her birthday as the voluntary at Evensong.

[Excerpt 3]

Bairstow's arrival at, and departure from, the Leeds appointment each brought forth from his pen significant works for the Parish Church choir to sing – from the late summer of his arrival came *Let all mortal flesh keep silence* of 1906; for some inexplicable unknown reason, it remained unpublished for nineteen years until 1925. This classic Introit for unaccompanied choir is a keystone of the twentieth century Anglican repertory; the score of this magnificent miniature remained with the Parish Church on its composer's departure to York Minster and it survives within a fine glass case provided for it by a generous donor in the early 1970s.

Bairstow's parting gift of a setting of the *Office for Holy Communion* – Responses to the Ten Commandments, fully choral Creed, Sanctus and Benedictus, Agnus Dei, and magnificent concluding Gloria – was issued by the London house of Novello. The thrilling self-assured organ introduction before the choir launches into the Gloria is without compare in the English choral repertoire of the Romantic period.

[Excerpt 4]

Earlier in Bairstow's time in Leeds, the same publishing concern had produced a number of fine anthems including the Eastertide *Sing ye to the Lord* and a deeply expressive setting of *If the Lord had not helped me*, composed following a serious illness from which the then Vicar of Leeds had not at first been expected to recover.

The main part of the duration of the First World War was led musically by Bairstow's immediate successor, Willoughby Williams, whose early career had involved a distinguished operatic career in Germany.[16] The complications of his family arrangements, his returning to Britain with a German wife, along with the shortage of quality adult male singers during the period of hostilities, meant the abandonment of choral services towards the end of the war. The difficulties of re-establishing things on a proper footing proved almost impossible and Williams left Leeds just a year after the Armistice, working subsequently in major London parishes and later within the Episcopal Church of the United States of America.

Williams was in his turn followed by Albert Charles Tysoe, from All Saints' Northampton.[17] He was to remain for seventeen years and the testimony of a collection of *Leeds Musical Festival* week service booklets produced triennially in the 1920s and 30s give splendid evidence of a golden period for the choir at that time. Clearly, Dr Tysoe worked within a framework of strict discipline for both boy and adult singers. Following its use at the Marriage of HRH The Prince of Wales to Lady Diana Spencer in 1981, Tysoe's fine descant to the hymn 'Praise my Soul the King of Heaven', almost certainly designed for use in connection with a Leeds Festival Service – as it is printed in one of the first booklets just mentioned – has achieved widespread performance, recording and adoption elsewhere ever since.

It is worth recording, of course, that Bairstow had planned and seen to fruition, a major, substantial and immensely successful, reconstruction of the Parish Church's fine organ by the leading twentieth-century firm of Harrison & Harrison from Durham. Completed by 1914, this instrument within a building of less than substantial natural acoustical resonance followed on from other major triumphs within churches of similar challenge – All Saints, Margaret Street, London and St Mary Redcliffe, Bristol, being other equally successful musical resources with a comparatively 'dry' acoustic.

The appointment of Melville Cook in 1937 was to prove of crucial importance to the revival of the choir after hostilities in another World War had ceased in 1945.[18] Very regular BBC Choral Evensong broadcasts attest to that. Dr Cook worked quickly and highly effectively to revive the choral fortunes of the Parish Church and this period saw further work by Harrison & Harrison on the organ, including, in the mid-1950s, the standardisation of the pitch of the instrument, to facilitate performance with orchestra and other solo musical resources, operating at what we now refer to in normal parlance as 'concert' pitch.

While it could with candour be admitted that neither of the first two successors to Bairstow seemed to have been drawn to composition in a major way, some fine examples of Melville Cook's craft as arranger and composer did come to light towards the end of the last century and the outset of the present one. A number of his works were privately printed here in Leeds, but others were taken up by Novello and Stainer & Bell in London as well as subsequently by Canadian publishing concerns. Dr Cook left Leeds for Hereford in 1956 and spent well over twenty in Toronto, Canada as Organist of the Metropolitan United Church there – a post held earlier in the last century [from 1917] with similar distinction by a former Leeds-based musician, Canterbury-born Herbert Austin Fricker, second City Organist and Choral Director of early twentieth-century Leeds Festivals.

Returning to his native Gloucestershire on retirement from his Canadian appointments, Dr Cook was a regular visitor to Leeds as a welcome guest of the family of Sydney Errington, an eminent Headingley musician, highly regarded as Principal Viola in Sir John Barbirolli's Hallé Orchestra in Manchester for many years.

Dr Cook's other Yorkshire appointments included the conductorship of Halifax Choral Society; in that capacity from 1937 to 1956, he continued the Parish Church's long connection with that famous Yorkshire choir that had begun generations previously.

Here is a glimpse of the real talent of Cook's musical concept. A superb arrangement of 'St Patrick's Breastplate' culminates in a magnificent final verse and the whole is every bit the equal of Stanford's more famous version produced for the ill-fated 1904 edition of *Hymns Ancient and Modern*.

[Excerpt 5]

There could perhaps be no better tribute to Dr Cook than a musician from an almost identical Midlands background being appointed to serve at Leeds in his stead. Following an interim appointment of Ronald

Perrin, later to serve with flair and distinction as Organist at Ripon Cathedral, Cook's successor, Dr Donald Hunt, arrived from Torquay with his wife and younger family in 1957.

If Cook's era had involved extensive live broadcasting of Leeds liturgies, that of Donald Hunt involved huge developments in the endeavour of recordings – at first vinyl long-playing records and, later, cassettes and CDs. The particular support of three major figures in the world of recording, Michael Smythe of *Vista* records, Harry Mudd of *Abbey* records, and Peter Hill [a former boy chorister here] and his Leeds-based firm of *Foxglove Audio*, was integral to the early widespread dissemination of recordings of both the organ and choir at Leeds Parish Church.

The fine organ was first heard on solo discs by Donald Hunt and by Melville Cook, who returned from Hereford to commit much fine music to the then fairly new medium of the long-playing record. Other recordings followed by Hunt's successor, Simon Lindley. Organ and choral recordings from the late 1960s and early 1970s enjoyed widespread critical acclaim and thus assisted in bringing the Parish Church and its musical foundation to regional, national and international notice.

In tandem with this programme of recording came the advent of the 'choir tours', held very regularly and often annually from 1968 for a period of some forty years or so, supported by a very thriving Choir Parents' Association and by the prodigious and often selfless generosity of generations of parishioners by means of social and fund-raising events of increasing ingenuity and imagination.

It is worth stating that all of this activity was undertaken by a choir without the benefit of a residential choir school, with the boys drawn from a wide range of local authority and independent schools within the Leeds metropolitan district and sometimes from further afield with often commendable levels of support and encouragement from the academic and teaching staff of such schools, support that was much valued and affirmed by the church authorities here as well as the chorister families. Likewise, within the ranks of the singing men, there were changes over recent decades brought about by the demands of full-time work on the one hand, and the benefits of a situation in the midst of what would today be referred to as a major educational *hub* on the other. Though there remained a small corpus of adults who had sung in the choir as trebles in their youth, this was – perhaps surprisingly – a comparatively modest numerical tally and a very small percentage of the overall personnel needed to sustain such an extensive choral foundation.

Donald Hunt, in office here from 1957 to 1975, showed early compositional gifts evincing real flair and originality and quickly established his composer credentials, at first locally, and later nationally and internationally. Much of his music had begun to attract leading publishers during his Leeds tenure and this creative endeavour increased during his subsequent time at Worcester Cathedral as Master of the Choristers and Organist between 1975 and 1996.

Along with Wesley and Bairstow, Hunt served the cause of creative music of his day well, not least with a number of extended works, of which *Hymnus Paschalis* is perhaps now the best known. He made many warmly welcomed return visits to Leeds following his move to his West Country roots and enjoyed a particularly fruitful association with the St Peter's Singers of Leeds, from 1977.

Our final musical snippet is the magnificent last movement of *Hymnus Paschalis* featuring the historic and noble hymn 'the strife is o'er, the battle done'.

[Excerpt 6]

1975 saw the appointment of Simon Lindley from St Albans Cathedral, whose tenure as a first-rate organist and charismatic choirmaster was to last for some 41 years.[19] Two years later, in 1977, the adult choir, St Peter's Singers of Leeds, was founded by lay clerk Harry Fearnley, and continues to flourish to this day. Lindley was appointed as its Director, a post that he held until 2020. St Peter's Singers were entirely Harry Fearnley's vision and the singers have brought an additional dimension to the breadth and scale of repertoire offered in the Minster, as the Oratorio Choir had done in previous generations. The tradition of daily choral services sung by the Parish Choir was sustained well into the twenty first century; and throughout most of the twentieth, the choir continued with its regular round of broadcasts and recordings. In 1996, then Sub-Organist Jonathan Lilley established a girls' choir which primarily led a service of Morning Worship on a Saturday morning, but which also became incorporated within the Yorkshire Cathedral Girls' Choir Festival, singing alongside the girls' ensembles of Bradford, Sheffield, Ripon, Wakefield and York Cathedrals each year. In the same way, the Parish Church Choir of Boys and Men was an integral part of the Yorkshire Three Choirs, whose annual October Festival saw them singing alongside the boys and men of Ripon and Wakefield Cathedrals in services and concerts.

Around the turn of the new millennium, a Choral Foundation Appeal was launched, attracting faithful and substantial support from committed parishioners, citizens, and donors including local businesses and charitable concerns near and far. These funds are in the care of the

Friends of the Music, whose stewardship of them allows so many of the musical expenses of the Parish to be covered, while allowing for medium and longer term planning.

In the latter years of the twentieth century it was becoming apparent that recruiting boys to sing in an inner-city church on an almost daily basis was becoming more and more of a challenge. The move of the Grammar School at Leeds to Alwoodley, several miles north of the city; the increasing demands of contemporary family and working life; ever busier traffic around chorister drop-off and pick-up times; and a widening demographic mix across the city and district, were all contributory factors. In 2015, the decision was taken by the then Rector, Canon Sam Corley, that the number of participating children in the choral programme was too slender to be sustainable, and the choirs of boys and girls were suspended that October.

Paul Dewhurst's appointment in 2016 as Organist and Director of Music saw the establishing of an adult chamber choir to lead Choral Evensong on Thursdays and two choral services each Sunday. Paul re-energised a choral scholarship programme that now sees students from the Universities of York and Leeds, as well as at Leeds Conservatoire, involved with the choir and gaining valuable musical experience alongside a healthy crop of experienced and tremendously loyal volunteer adult singers, many of whom had served as Lay Clerks in the Parish Choir. The result, the current Minster Choir, is a strong choir of around 30 members which is well-balanced, well-integrated and able to work at pace and sing a great breadth of repertoire.

The global pandemic of 2020, out of which we are still slowly emerging, led to the suspension of all choral services from the 15 March 2020, just three weeks after the appointment of Alexander Woodrow to the Organist and Director of Music post. Since then, the past 18 months have seen something of a stop-start nature to the music making at the Minster, dictated by national restrictions as well as the church's rightful desire to keep its congregation, staff and volunteers safe. While an array of different cantors and vocal quartets have been able to lead services, tomorrow, Sunday 12 September, in fact sees the first Sunday in 2021 to have services sung by the full Minster Choir. We hope, to paraphrase our Prime Minister, that this progress is of an 'irreversible' nature, this being in fact the third such attempted restart in the past year.

Before concluding, we will hear David performing the Choral Song of S. S. Wesley played on the superb Minster organ. It was a work written $c.$1832–4, well before his move to Leeds in 1842.

[Excerpt 7]

So, in 2021, the musical foundation and resources here at Leeds Minster look markedly different from the choir documented in 1818 during Vicar Fawcett's tenure, but the aspiration is still the same: 'to have a good choir', to quote Dr Hook. Indeed the move from the traditional male choir to a mixed, adult one was seamless and while the break with tradition is, in some ways, regrettable, the adult choir has produced many outstanding performances of an ambitious repertoire spanning six centuries, performances that would have been challenging for the male choir.

Thanks to our choir members and the supporters of the music here, and despite emerging from a global pandemic, the Minster's renowned musical tradition continues to flourish. Dr Hook believed that the choral service was 'one of the finest expressions of faith'; he would be proud of the legacy he bequeathed to Leeds.

Notes

1. Letter from Hook to W. P. Wood Esq, 10 February 1841, quoted in W. R. W. Stephens, *The Life and Letters of Walter Farquhar Hook*, 2 vols (London, 1879) II, 124.
2. No-one seeking the context and history of music at what in 2012 became Leeds Minster can fail to acknowledge an immense debt to Donald Webster, boy chorister in the 1930s and Sub-Organist, 1962–8. *See* Donald Webster, *'Parish' Past and Present; 275 Years of Leeds Parish Church Music* (Leeds, 1988). He gathered around himself a small working group to assist in the enterprise, thus leaving future generations, including our own, very much in his debt.
3. For Wesley, see Peter Horton, *Samuel Sebastian Wesley: a Life* (Oxford, 2004).
4. See John Jebb, *The Choral Service of the United Church of England and Ireland* (London, 1843).
5. For Frederick Oakeley, see Raymond Beazley, 'Oakeley, Frederick' in Sidney Lee (ed.), *Dictionary of National Biography*, vol. 41 (London, 1895).
6. Anon., *Seven Sermons Preached at the Consecration and Re-Opening of the Parish Church of Leeds* (Leeds, 1841). As well as the sermons, the book contains a lengthy Introduction describing the history of the church, the music performed at the services and a list of all the clergy attending.
7. Harry W. Dalton, *Anglican Resurgence under W. F. Hook in Early Victorian Leeds* (Leeds, 2002), 59–60.
8. Webster, *Parish*, 22.
9. *Leeds Intelligencer*, 30 November 1826.

10. Nigel Yates, *Anglican Ritual in Victorian Britain 1830–1910* (Oxford, 1999), 57, quoting B. Rainbow, *The Choral Revival in the Anglican Church* (London, 1970), 3, 308. On different pages, Rainbow quotes *Leeds Mercury*, 26 November 1826 and 26 November 1828. However, on neither date was the *Mercury* – a weekly newspaper – printed and despite extensive searches, Rainbow's quotations have not been found. Nevertheless, a heated vestry meeting did take place on 23 November 1826 which was recorded in the other Leeds newspaper, the *Leeds Intelligence,* of 30 November 1826. It records one of the protesters as saying 'the practice [of robed choristers] came from a popish source' while another claimed 'to see six men in white gowns, chaunting the praise of God for a piece of bread was, to his mind, one of the most offensive things in the world'. What is clear is that, in 1826, a robed choir unquestionably existed. See also *Leeds Mercury*, 24 November 1827, reporting another heated vestry meeting on this subject.

11. E. Kitson Clark, *A History and Description of St Peter's Church, Leeds* (London, n.d.), 44. See also Leeds Mercury, 24 November 1827.

12. '[Hook] on his arrival, found the surplices in rags and the service books in tatters'. Stephens, *Hook*, I, 374.

13. A. F. Barker in *Yorkshire Weekly Post*, 18 August 1929.

14. For Donald Hunt, see Robert Cummings, 'Donald Hunt' in AllMusic, accessed 16 February 2022.

15. For Bairstow, see Francis Jackson, *Blessed City: The Life and Work of Edward C. Bairstow, 1874–1946* (York, 1996).

16. For Williams, see Webster, *Parish*, 81–92.

17. For Tyso, see Webster, *Parish*, 93–7.

18. For Cook see Watkins Shaw and Roy Massey, *The Organists and Organs of Hereford Cathedral* (Hereford, 2005).

19. For Lindley, see Maggie Smith and Robert Humphries, *Dictionary of Composers for the Church in Great Britain and Ireland* (London, 1977).

7.

'The dim religious light cast by the many painted windows': the Glazing of the New Leeds Parish Church

MICHAEL SWIFT

The quotation in the title is part of a longer one from Dr Hook's first biographer that caught the effect made by the stained glass windows on the minds of the congregation at the newly consecrated Leeds Parish Church in 1841. 'The dim religious light cast by the many painted windows – the aspect of the whole is very solemn and striking even from an artistic point of view.'[1]

In recent decades much valuable work has been undertaken to re-assess the status and significance of Dr Hook's and Robert Dennis Chantrell's building.[2] It is, however, surprising that so little attention has been paid to over 40 stained glass windows that were inserted from 1841 onwards.[3] The purpose of this paper is to show that a close analysis of the form and functions of these windows adds a new dimension to the current narratives on the church's place in the development of the Gothic Revival, as well as the church's relationship with its congregation and the wider community of Leeds.

It is essential to remember that the planning and rebuilding of Leeds Parish Church under Hook predated the first issue of *The Ecclesiologist*. This has been proved to be relevant when Chantrell's architectural vision is assessed, but it is also important to remember that decisions on the use of stained glass also preceded the Ecclesiological advocacy of this artistic medium. Hook's positive attitude towards the symbolic effect of stained glass was shown as early as 1829, when one of his first acts at Holy Trinity, Coventry, was to fill the Chancel east window with stained glass as part of a general High Church re-ordering of the interior.[4] It is therefore consistent with his High Church views that at least 22 stained glass windows were inserted for the consecration of his new Leeds Parish Church in 1841.[5]

We are so used today to the idea that donating a stained glass window is a suitable memorial, that it is something of a shock to realise that this practice started only in the 1840s. James Markland advocated it at Oxford in 1842 as an alternative to the ever-larger stone memorials of the Georgian period,[6] and the Beckett memorial window in the Lady Chapel at Leeds predated his seminal paper by a year.[7] Memorial

Fig. 7.1: Chancel East (part of central light), 'Crucifixion and the Apostles', 1841, assembled by John Summers. (© Jonathan Cooke)

windows to members of the Blayds family of Oulton,[8] and Antony Titley of Wortley Lodge followed quickly.[9]

The glazing in the first decades of the new church reveals not only the intentions of Hook, Chantrell and the patrons, but also their degree of success and failure. The early congregations would have been profoundly impressed by the colour and iconography, which in itself was Hook's vigorous riposte to Evangelical Anglican and Nonconformist attitudes to such embellishments. Standing at the crossing, the eastward facing worshippers had an unimpeded view of the high altar, raised on an impressive flight of seven steps, and surmounted by a dazzling display of stained glass in the sanctuary apse.[10] The figurative old Flemish glass of the apostles re-assembled in the sanctuary by John Summers was particularly singled out by contemporary commentators (Fig. 7.1).[11] This central window's style and colours were matched, with debatable success, by Thomas Wilmshurst of London in the adjoining sanctuary apse windows four years later.[12] The figurative portrayals of apostles with their attributes, together with the iconography of Wilmshurst's windows – the Crucifixion, narrative panels of the Gospel story and the life of the patronal saint, St Peter –were entirely appropriate to celebrate the sacrament of Eucharist with colour and light in this discrete space.

When the worshippers at the crossing turned to the west they were faced with an entirely different artistic and religious experience. The upper west window of 1841 – donated by the 25 Patrons – and the lower west window of 1856 – donated by the 13 Founders – were by David Evans of Shrewsbury.[13] With the exception of two small narrative panels, the shields of the church's Patrons throughout are portrayed with the same civic pride as the enameled painted windows in the earlier church.[14] The iconography of these two west windows is almost entirely secular, and in total contrast to the sacred subject-matter of the sanctuary east windows. The sole exceptions to the armorials were the two narrative panels of 'Christ summoning little children' and 'Christ's baptism in the River Jordan'. These were the gift of the Founder Henry Skelton, in lieu of his coat of arms 'of which he did not approve'(Fig. 7.2).[15] It is ironic that these panels are the only ones that relate to the sacramental function of the baptistery at the foot of the window, and that they are entirely overshadowed by the civic themes of the rest of the window.

Many of the early windows were in a decorative artistic style. Some were mosaic pattern, somewhat unsophisticated in manufacture and design, as in the northwest window below the gallery which included, within the mosaic, the Royal Arms and those of the Archbishop of York reused from the old church. This mosaic style includes the so-called 'Penny Window' in the City of Leeds Room, paid for by the donations from the poor of the city and installed in 1841. Contemporary reports show some doubt on their quality: 'The mosaic windows are made out of old fragments of broken glass, stained and painted ; they are all too glaring, but will be much improved by the smoke and dust with which in the course of time they will be covered.'[16]

Fig. 7.2: West Window (lower part), Founders' armorials with 'Suffer Little Children' and 'Baptism of Christ', 1856, by David Evans. (© Jonathan Cooke)

A more sophisticated decorative style was to be found in the coloured geometric patterned windows, many of which still survive in the gallery. These brightly coloured and intricately patterned windows were of a higher quality than the mosaic windows. Later references indicate that decorative windows were even more extensive, but there is no documentary evidence to date their insertions other than from 1841 to the renovations in the 1860s.[17]

Hook's desire to fill as many windows as possible with stained glass was part of a series of innovations that he introduced to the internal arrangement and lavish furnishings of his new church, a reflection of his decidedly High Anglican preferences.[18] Why therefore were some of the patterned windows of inferior quality in design and execution? A study of the accounts for the re-building affords one plausible explanation.[19] In the total building costs of almost £30,000, the sum spent on the stained glass windows was a mere £272. 2s. 3d., excluding Thomas Blayds' donation of the sanctuary windows and the Beckett memorial window (£2,000 according to the *Leeds Intelligencer*).[20] A breakdown of the £272 reveals that Evans was paid £32. 2s. 0d. for his west window; glass merchants (Heaps and Lonsdale) received £32. 7s. 0d.; John Bower, jnr. of Hunslet – the only recorded glass-stainer in the current Leeds trade Directory[21] – was paid £31. 11s. 9d.; and the remaining £164. 3s. 0d. went to Garlick, a local firm of engineers and plumbers, who were responsible for the actual fitting of the windows. In later years, Hook made many references to the outstanding debt incurred by the rebuilding of the church.[22] The most obvious explanation for the style and quality of the decorative patterned windows was that Hook's desire to enhance the High Church ambience with as much stained glass as possible was not matched by sufficient funds or donors.

This tension between didactic and decorative intent is partially resolved by a closer examination of the geometric patterned windows that have survived in the south gallery. Professor Curl maintains that such geometric figures were of great symbolic significance, and as such were a direct link with the art of the medieval stained glass craftsmen.[23] Forms such as squares, circles, equilateral triangles (interlinked or associated with other figures), and *vesica piscis* are all present in these windows.[24] In medieval glass designs, Curl maintains that such forms were spiritually the symbols of man's need to express his relationship with the living world. They were therefore appropriate in a Victorian High Church context, as an expression of aspirations to spiritual things.[25] Also, the mandala forms present in these windows echo systems for proportioning buildings, a subject that deeply concerned Chantrell at this time, as he strove to give architectural form to Hook's

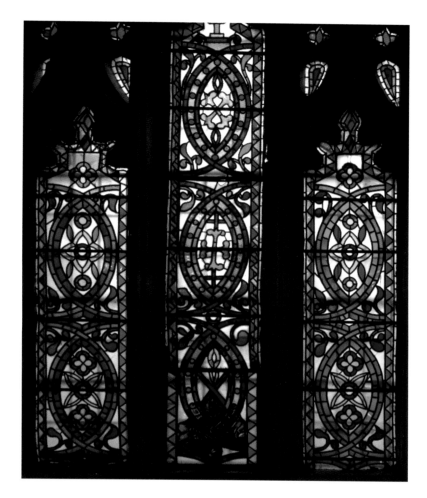

Fig. 7.3: South Gallery 2, geometric patterns, 1841, probably by John Bower, junior, of Hunslet, Leeds. (© Jonathan Cooke)

vision of a pre-Reformation tradition (Fig. 7.3).[26] It is important to stress that such symbolism was far more widely perceived and understood in early-Victorian architecture, art and literature than it is in the twenty-first century. It can be argued that the local manufacturer of these decorative windows produced a statement about the ecclesiastical use of stained glass in a High Church context. Within five years, such symbolic patterns were considered obsolete for full-sized windows in the ongoing Ecclesiological debate concerning the suitability, form and substance of stained glass.[27]

To summarize so far, the well-known local saying about ritual, that 'there's High Church and Low Church and Leeds Parish Church', applies equally to its stained glass.[28] In 1841, the earliest examples of High Church stained glass in the town were inserted just seven months before the start of Ecclesiological discussions on the nature, function and acceptability of Anglican stained glass.[29] Whilst Summer's re-assembly of old glass in the sanctuary can be seen as a visual representation of Hook's Higher ideals, the remaining windows present a paradox.[30] The 1811 painted St Peter window, reinserted in the south aisle from the south transept of the old Parish Church, had nothing in common either technically or artistically with the merits of medieval mosaic-glass techniques advocated by both Pugin and Ecclesiologists. Just as the iconography of this full-length painted glass figure was of an earlier age, so also were the armorials in David Evans' west windows, and Ward & Nixon's Beckett memorial in the lady chapel east window.[31] There is thus a tension between the archaic iconography of these windows and the radical purpose that they were intended to fulfil within the context of the new Higher architecture and ritual. It appears that in 1841 the effect of having immediate light and colour was more important to Hook than the actual iconography.

This brings us to the most important aspect of the glazing of Hook's new church. We have focused on the contemporary worshippers' response to the east and west windows from their viewpoint at the crossing. The church has a cruciform plan with four major windows at the cardinal points, so what about the south and north transept windows? The answer is of course that the south transept window is largely obscured by the organ, and the north transept window has remained plain glazed since 1841.[32] There is therefore no evidence of an overall didactic plan for the windows to make them an integral part of the architecture and the liturgy. It was a missed opportunity, one that ironically was seized when the neighbouring St Saviour's church was consecrated, only four years after St Peter's. A completely newly built major church offered a 'blank sheet of paper' to both the architect and the religious authorities. Thus by the 1870s some of the largest commissions for contemporary stained glass were awarded to buildings such as the new cathedrals at Truro in Cornwall and Melbourne in Australia, both of which had elaborate integrated didactic schemes conceived *before* the foundation stones were laid.[33]

The absence of a didactic scheme had religious, artistic and social consequences. The choice of iconography primarily came down to donor preference. This often resulted in the repetition of popular favourite themes throughout the same building. Figures of saints could be chosen to match the name of the dedicatee, as in Saints John and Anne in John and Ann Heaton's window, and St Thomas in that of Thomas Tennant.[34] Donors also could show a preference for a particular glass studio, resulting in artistic clashes between adjacent windows. Often the iconography was chosen because the subject matter was appropriate to the dedicatee, as in the healing scenes in North Gallery 7,[35] for Francis

Sharpe (surgeon) who died of fever whilst administering to the poor in Leeds in 1847,[36] and the adjacent window of similar healing scenes dedicated to Samuel Smith, Senior Surgeon at Leeds General Infirmary.[37] The lack of a didactic scheme can result in a donor appropriating a particular space in the building. North Gallery 5 is a memorial to Ralph and Frances Markland, 'over the family pew'.[38] Another example of such consequences of donor preference is seen in the Rooke memorial window above the north-west gallery.[39] 'The Ascension' is portrayed in vivid colours totally at odds with the glass in its neighbouring windows, and the subject is inappropriate for this position.

Such incongruities resulting from a lack of a comprehensive didactic scheme are also illustrated in South Aisle 2, where the Jacob Wright enamel-painted St Peter window of 1811 from the old church was re-inserted. Not only is the enamel-painted light artistically at odds with all the rest of the new stained glass windows, but also the lights on either side of Saints Thomas and James the Less seem completely out of place. In fact, these were originally part of the clerestory didactic scheme at the nearby St Saviours church.[40] They were removed from that church prior to 1872, and rather crudely inserted next to St Peter in the Parish Church (Fig. 7.4).[41]

Fig. 7.4: South Aisle 2: 'St Peter', 1811, by Jacob Wright, removed from the old Parish Church; 'St Thomas' and 'St James the Less', 1847, by Michael O'Connor, originally in the clerestory of St Saviour's church, Leeds. (© Jonathan Cooke)

Fig. 7.5: Sanctuary South 1, panel showing the typological pairing of 'Moses Striking the Rock' together with 'The Baptism of Christ' (Gott memorial window), 1862, by William Wailes. (© Jonathan Cooke)

Further incongruities are seen in the typological Benjamin Gott memorial window in the sanctuary.[42] This is an elaborate design of six panels of Old Testament subjects chosen as types to six antitype subjects from the Gospels (Fig. 7.5). This strong religious content is rather lost in a window tucked into the corner of the sanctuary and flanked by the Titley and Hartley memorial windows. All three were inserted over a period of seventeen years (1845–62), the iconography of the earlier windows having no connection with the typology of the Gott window.[43] The manufacturers – Thomas Wilmshurst of London, William Wailes of Newcastle and William Warrington of London – were all highly respected studios of the early Gothic Revival. They all had their own individual styles, and besides the lack of religious coherence, there is a lack of artistic unity which might be expected when their windows are in the same corner of the building.

A breakdown of insertion dates of stained glass windows in Leeds Parish Church, excluding all patterned windows:

1840s – 8 windows;
1850s – 3 windows;
1860s – 15 windows;
1870s – 2 windows.

Two further stained glass windows were inserted in 1905 and 1951.[44]

Half of the church's full stained-glass windows were inserted in the 1860s after the church's renovation.[45] The 1860s saw the emergence of new studios such as Clayton & Bell whose 'Life of St Paul' in the chancel is one of the best in the church,[46] while Heaton, Butler & Bayne produced the striking 'Acts of Charity' window.[47] Michael O'Connor remained a popular choice for donors.[48] However, studios that followed the Pre-Raphaelites and the Arts and Crafts traditions were not chosen by donors in this church, in contrast to elsewhere in Leeds.[49] Today the windows of Leeds Parish Church seem to be conservative in glazing terms, but this is to ignore Hook's radical approach to stained glass from 1840 onwards. A closer look at three areas within the church reveals further points of interest.

The glazing of the south gallery retains some of the original 1841 geometric patterned windows. The one exception is the 1909 window of the 'Blessed Virgin Mary with Saints Elizabeth and Hilda'. This was made by the local studio of Chas E. Steel, and is dedicated to Chas E. Steel senior: it is a fascinating example of how tastes in stained glass colouring and style were to develop in the fifty years after the 1860 renovation. One question that remains to be answered is why the 1841 geometric patterned windows survived in this gallery, and were not replaced by full stained glass in later decades.

The glazing of the north gallery is in complete contrast. Here only two of the original 1841 geometric windows survived being replaced with full stained glass, but only to be replaced by plain glazing to make the gallery lighter in the twentieth century.[50] The remaining gallery windows are all of quality and interest. The first is a 1874 Clayton & Bell memorial to Joseph Mason Tennant,[51] showing 'Martha and Mary', 'The call to Lazarus' and 'Lazarus rising from the tomb'. This was a very popular iconographical subject for a memorial window in the second half of the nineteenth century. The fourth gallery window is the aforementioned Heaton memorial, and the only window in the church from the prestigious Lavers, Barraud & Westlake studio. Three windows of 1866–8 are by the Michael O'Connor studio: the ways the iconography of windows 7 and 8 reflect the dedicatee's professions has already been noted. North Gallery 5, the Markland memorial, is a rare typological iconography for the church.[52] North Gallery 6 is very unusual in that it was made by 'the Revd H. F. St John, curate to Dr Woodford, fond of painting subjects for stained glass, of which he had executed several. He had them burnt by a professional and practical artist'.[53] He was one of a number of Victorian clergy who were talented amateur glass painters and in some cases makers also. Before leaving the north gallery, it is worth noting that after 1860 this gallery was very popular for donors of full stained glass memorial windows, in marked contrast to the south gallery. This is the opposite to the normal preference for well-lit south facing windows over the north facing windows with no direct sunlight. Could this be because the north gallery pews were more desirable as they provided a better position for viewing the pulpit and sermons, and as we have seen, in at least one case the window was 'above the family pew'? Certainly, these were the most prestigious pews with rents higher than those in the south gallery.

In many ways the story of the glazing of Leeds Parish Church is encapsulated in the stained glass of the Lady Chapel (originally the Ante-Chapel).[54] The first stage was the windows that were installed for the 1841 consecration. These must have been similar to the geometric patterned windows that were in place in the nave galleries and the chancel clerestory. Despite being regarded by some as 'of excellent design and brilliant colours' and 'very elegant, brilliant and elaborate geometric designs',[55] they were deemed to 'insufficiently harmonize'[56] with the narrative stained glass memorial windows that quickly replaced them after 1860. The exception to survive was the 1841 Ward & Nixon armorial Beckett memorial in the east end of the chapel.

The windows in this second stage of the glazing of the Lady Chapel after the 1860 renovation were donated by the families of the original founders.[57] This chapel, together with the Sanctuary and the north gallery, were obviously the most sought after parts of the church for placing memorial windows and attracted the richest donors. Once again, Michael O'Connor was the favoured studio for the three windows in the north wall, the exception being the preference for the studio of William Wailes for the Beckett window in Lady Chapel North 1.[58] The iconography in each window is consistent,[59] but the absence of a master scheme results in muddled chronology when they are viewed as a sequence. The O'Connor memorial windows for the Hall and Tennant dedicatees are all crowded scenes with heavy borders and headings of stylised vegetative motifs in dark reds and blues, a colour scheme that was continued into the traceries.

This final stage of glazing in the Lady Chapel takes us back to the 'dim, religious light' of the opening paragraph, and the various measures taken in the twentieth century to remedy what was obviously deemed to be a serious problem. The church's windows as a whole remain a veritable time capsule of the stained glass revival of the middle of the nineteenth century, but this Victorian vision was adapted during the twentieth century. Actually, this process had started after the 1860 renovation: the four windows in the east and west transepts above the arches into the nave and choir were 'pierced for the express purpose of throwing light upon the pulpit and reading desk, the whole interior being now rather gloomy in consequence of so many painted windows.'[60] However, the major alterations to the Victorian glazing were undertaken in the 1950s, with the 'removal of existing windows of Victorian glass [replaced by] plain leaded glass to admit more light to the church.'[61] What remains of Lady Chapel North 1 was a direct result of such intervention. This Beckett memorial window made by William Wailes in 1860 had all its backgrounds and borders in both the main lights and tracery replaced with plain glass to admit more light. This was a time when appreciation of Victorian stained glass was at its lowest ebb, and the destruction of the artistic integrity of the window was regarded then as an acceptable price to pay for more light. This is even more unfortunate in the Maude and Chorley memorial windows in the City of Leeds Room, where the subjects 'float' in midair, whilst the unaltered tracery shows what rich colours from the original has been lost.

This paper has attempted to locate the church's glazing within the context of the new church's first decades by reading the windows in the context of Victorian Anglicanism and culture. It is work in progress.[62] Further research, for example on the windows' donors and dedicatees,[63] and the church Trustees with their involvement in the civic and commercial life of Leeds, could well provide a rich source of socio-economic information that would add greatly to the narratives of the church's interaction with its congregation and the wider civic life of the town in the nineteenth century. This paper has shown that the stained glass, like the building's architecture, was ahead of its time in the year of the church's consecration, but within a short number of years, had been overtaken by the trends and fashions often led by the Ecclesiologists.

Notes

1. W. R. W. Stephens, *Life and Letters of Walter Farquhar Hook*, 2 vols (London, 1878), I, 169.
2. Christopher Webster, *The rebuilding of Leeds Parish Church 1837–41, and its place in the Gothic Revival* (London, 1994); Christopher Webster, *R. D. Chantrell (1793–1872) and the architect of a lost generation*, (Reading, 2010).
3. The only recent attention that has been paid to the fittings of Leeds Parish Church are: Margaret Pullan, *The Monuments of the parish church of St Peter-at-Leeds*, (Leeds, 2007); Michael G. Swift, 'An examination of the development of stained glass windows in the Anglican churches of Leeds 1841–1860', unpublished M. A. thesis, Trinity & All Saints, University of Leeds, 1999.
4. Stephens, *Hook*, I, 169.
5. Stephens, *Hook*, II, 89. Webster, *Leeds Parish Church*, 19–20.
6. At the Oxford Architectural Society.
7. Made by Ward & Nixon of London, 1841.
8. Sanctuary Apse left and right lights, made by Wilmshurst of London. *The Builder*, 23 January 1847, 43; R. W. Moore, *A History of the Parish Church of Leeds* (London, 1877), 39; J. Rusby, *History of Leeds Parish Church* (Leeds, 1897), 89.
9. Sanctuary East, also probably made by Wilmshurst.
10. G. W. O. Addleshaw and F. Etchells, *The Architectural Setting for Anglican Worship* (London, 1948), 210–22.
11. *Leeds Intelligencer*, 8 May, 1841. There may be some doubt about the provenance of this older glass.
12. *Leeds Intelligencer*, 20 July, 1844.
13. Moore, History, 39. Rusby, *History*, 90.
14. There are numerous fragments of armorials from the old church incorporated in patterned windows above the gallery, and the enamel painted style is preserved in the St Peter panel in the south aisle window below the gallery.
15. Moore, *History*, 40.
16. *Leeds Intelligencer*, 25 August, 1841. A remarkable sequence of 'medley' windows has survived at Chantrell's nearby St Paul, Shadwell, consecrated in the following year.

17. *The Builder*, 22 September 1866, 386, refers to the insertion of the final pictorial stained glass window in north Lady Chapel (the earlier ones dated 1862–4), 'replacing one that did not sufficiently harmonise with those adjoining'. Moore, *History*, 40, indicates that the northwest gallery window was filled with geometric patterns, but these were removed by a 1951 Faculty (Ripon Diocesan Registry) to admit more light to the stairs.

18. Addleshaw and Etchells, *Architectural Setting*, pps. 210–18; Webster, *Leeds Parish Church*, 20–22.

19. West Yorkshire Archive Service (Leeds District Archives) 41/5, 45–58

20. *Leeds Intelligencer*, 2 October 1841.

21. White's *Directory of Leeds and the West Riding*, (Sheffield, 1841).

22. Stephens, *Hook*, II, 124, 137, 176.

23. James Stevens Curl, *Victorian Architecture - its practical aspects* (Newton Abbot, 1973), 39.

24. The vesica piscis is a mathematical shape formed by the intersection of two circles of equal radius so that each circle passes through the centre of the other one. The vesica piscis is sometimes used as a proportioning system in architecture, in particular in Gothic architecture.

25. Curl, *Victorian Architecture*, 41.

26. For Chantrell's interest in the subject, see Christopher Webster, "True Masonic Principles": a mid-nineteenth century alternative to "True Principles"' in *Ecclesiology Today*, 18, 1999, 1–5.

27. *The Ecclesiologist*, 4, n.s. 1, 1845, 200–203; Revd Drake in *The Builder*, 25 March 1843, 84–5; Bishop of Norwich in *The Builder*, 31 May 1845, 263.

28. Webster, *Leeds Parish Church*, 30.

29. *The Ecclesiologist*, 2, 1842–3, 72.

30. *Leeds Intelligencer*, 25 August 1841; *The Builder*, 23 January, 1847, 43; Moore, History, 38, 'collected and reconstructed, &c. by John Summers'; Rusby, *History*, 81, 'Old stained glass collected on the continent by Mr. John Summers'. In the 1842 *Directory*, John Summers is listed as 'artist' at 20 Park Row. There may be some doubt about the provenance of this older glass.

31. Moore, *History*, 47, 'seven coats of Beckett arms, worked in with geometric and mosaic work.' Window removed in twentieth century.

32. Despite plans at one stage to insert a memorial window to Hook.

33. Michael G. Swift, *The stained glass of Truro Cathedral – a Victorian vision fulfilled*, 2017, https://www.cornishstainedglass.org.uk/mgstc/. The companion project, Michael G. Swift and Dorothea Rowse *The stained glass of Melbourne cathedral – Truro's antipodean cousin* is in preparation.

34. Heaton window North Gallery 4 by Heaton, Butler & Bayne, 1862, and Tennant window Lady Chapel North 3 by Michael O'Connor 1853. Moore, *History*, 45; Rusby, *History*, 99.

35. The window nomenclature used throughout is numbering windows from east to west.

36. From window's inscription, made by Michael O'Connor, 1868.

37. *The Builder*, 3 October 1868, 739, also made by Michael O'Connor, 1868.

38. *The Builder*, 22 September 1866, 386.

39. *The Builder*, 26 February 1875, 580, by J. B. Capronnier of Brussels. See also Sarah Jarron, 'Capronnier's Yorkshire Legacy', *Journal of the British Society of Master Glass Painters*, xxxviii, 2014, 12–36.

40. J. & R. Cooke & M. Swift, 'The Clerestory windows of St. Saviour's Leeds', *Journal of … Painters*, xxi, 1997, 41–3.

41. Cooke and Swift, 'clerestory windows', 42.' These are incorporated into a much larger opening, built out in unpainted glass and eighteenth century painted fragments worked into a crude design'.

42. *The Builder*, 19 April 1862, 282. First window in the south wall, made by William Wailes of Newcastle in 1862 to designs by E. M. Barry.

43. The Titley window's subjects are 'Jesus before Pilate', ' St. John', 'Jesus and St. Thomas'. The Hartley window's subjects are (Left) 'St. John Evangelist', above 'Martha and Mary', above 'Distribution of Talents'; (Centre) 'Blessed Virgin Mary' above 'Jesus wept' above 'Reckoning of Talents'; (Right) 'St. John the Baptist' above 'Raising of Lazarus' above 'Reward of Talents'.

44. See Swift, 'An Examination', Appendix C, 48a–c.

45. For the first phase of the 'renovation', see *The Builder*, 19, 1861, 621, 772, 792, 812.

46. *Ripon Diocesan Kalendar*, 1868, p. 173; Moore, *History*, 43. Rusby, *History*, 97. Sanctuary North, Clayton & Bell memorial window to William Gott, the father of the then current vicar (inserted 1867).

47. Moore, *History*, p. 41; Rusby, *History*, 94; City of Leeds Room, west door, Heaton Butler and Bayne memorial to William, Annie and Emil Booker (1863). This is in the characteristic colours of this studio one year before their west window at Bradford Cathedral.

48. At least six windows in the Lady Chapel and north gallery (1853–68) and the reinserted St Saviour windows in the south aisle.

49. William Morris windows were inserted in the nearby St Saviour's (1870) and Mill Hill Chapel (1875), and at St Peter's Bramley (1875).

50. North Gallery 2, dedicated to Robert John Saunders (Inspector of Factories), died 1852, and North Gallery 3, dedicated to William Whyatt (assistant curate, army chaplain in Crimea), inscriptions remain only.

51. Ripon Diocesan Kalendar, 1875, 190; Moore, *History*, 46; Rusby, *History*, 100.

52. Moore, *History*, 47, 'Abraham, type of princely power; Melchisedec, type of high priest; Isaac, type of sacrifice, all types of our Blessed Lord.'

53. Moore, *History*, 47. H. Tom Kupper in Carol Bennett (ed.), *Stained Glass of Lincoln Cathedral* (London, 2012), 88–89 on probably the most famous of these Victorian amateurs, Revd A. S. Sutton and his brother Revd F.H. Sutton. The Revd William Willimott did the whole glazing in two of his Cornwall churches, St Michael Caerhays see Michael G Swift https://www.cornishstainedglass.org.uk/mgsdb/church.xhtml?churchid=250 , and Quethiock https://www.cornishstainedglass.org.uk/mgsdb/church.xhtml?churchid=186

54. Moore, *History*, 42. This term was still in use in 1873.

55. Moore, *History*, 45.

56. *The Builder*, 22 September 1866, 386, refers to the insertion of the final pictorial stained glass window in north Lady Chapel (the earlier ones dated 1862–4) 'replacing one that did not sufficiently harmonise with those adjoining'.

57. Lady Chapel 1, Beckett; 2, Hall; 3–4, Tennant.

58. Moore, History, p. 43. Rusby, *History*, 96.

59. 1. Crucifixion, Resurrection and Ascension; 2. Three healing miracles; 3. Crucifixion and two post-Resurrection revelations; 4. Two early Gospel narratives and two Passion episodes.

60. Moore, *History*, 47.

61. Ripon Diocesan Faculty, 1951, this also involved the removal of geometric pattern windows in the south chancel.

62. The author acknowledges with grateful thanks the help and assistance of the following in the preparation of this article: Mark Charter, Ann Clark, Jonathan and Ruth Cooke, Charlotte Evers and Judith Whitehouse.

63. Of the 25 Patrons whose arms appear in the 1841 West window, twelve of the families contributed memorial windows to the church in the following decades.

Appendix:

Dr Hook's Leeds Successors, 1859–1916

JANET DOUGLAS

Before Dr Hook's election, Leeds' vicars were local men belonging to families well-established in the town and its vicinity. With one exception, those who followed him were not, they were outsiders with little to no acquaintance with the North of England. Educated at public school followed by undergraduate studies at either Oxford of Cambridge, this might well have given them the aura of authority as did their black frock coats and top hats, but this hardly prepared them for the experience of an industrial town with its squalid conditions and teeming working classes. Nevertheless Leeds had its attractions; after the distinguished incumbency of Dr Hook, its vicariate came to be regarded as one of the most important in the country and a stepping stone to episcopal office. This was to have a significant effect on the way nominations were made in Leeds, normally vested in 25 church trustees, all local men, but when the previous vicar had been elevated to a bishopric, this right of appointment was transferred to the Crown (i.e. the Prime Minister). As five of Hook's seven successors became bishops, this diluted any local control over vicariate nomination. All the incumbents were High Churchmen though to different degrees. Only one, Edward Stuart Talbot, might be considered an Anglo-Catholic. All were Conservatives by political persuasion. Their strengths and accomplishments varied, some were famed for their preaching, some were academic clerics whilst others, having previously served as curates, were practiced in their pastoral roles. Although Hook's Vicarage Act of 1844 had divided the Leeds Parish into 25 new parishes, the vicar of Leeds remained responsible for over a dozen different livings and therefore their churchmanship had consequences for the whole of Leeds Anglicanism.

James Atlay (1817–94), vicar 1859–68

Born into a clerical family in Northamptonshire and after an education at Oakham School and St John's College, Cambridge, James Atlay was ordained in 1842 and for three years served as a curate at Warsop in Nottinghamshire. In 1847 he became a fellow and tutor at St John's College and was appointed vicar of Madingley. A scholarly cleric, Atlay had very little parochial experience when he was chosen to become Vicar of Leeds in 1859 where he continued Hook's work but avoided theological controversies being neither of High Church nor Low Church persuasion. One of the weaknesses of Hook's vicariate was that he was not particularly business-like or interested in financial matters, Atlay excelled in both. In 1862 he introduced a weekly offertory, established the Church Extension Society on a sound financial footing and raised the funds for the building of the Leeds Church Institute in Albion Place to provide a central focus for Leeds Anglicanism. If this suggests strategic preoccupations, Altay never neglected his more mundane pastoral responsibilities, he was an assiduous home visitor of the squalid areas around his Parish church. One poor woman later told Cosmo Lang when he was curate at Leeds, 'Eh, but I liked Jeems Atlay, he was a right homely man'. In 1868 Dr Atlay left Leeds to become Bishop of Hereford.

James Russell Woodford (1820–85), vicar 1868–73

An only child brought up by a widowed mother in Henley on Thames, James Woodford was what today is known as a late developer. However a legacy from a distant relative allowed him to take up a scholarship at Pembroke College, Cambridge where he was an early member of the Cambridge Camden Society (from 1845 known as the Ecclesiology Society). On leaving Cambridge his first employment was as a school master at the Anglican Bishop's College in Bristol, and it was here that he was ordained, and subsequently appointed to various minor clerical posts in the Bristol area. Despite his retiring disposition, he developed into a powerful preacher which brought him to the attention of Samuel Wilberforce, Bishop of Oxford and it was he who championed the advancement of his career. Appointed to Leeds in 1868, his preaching prowess brought immense crowds back to the Parish church and it was said that the line of carriages began at the church gates and continued well down East Street. A High churchman convinced of the beauty of holiness, it was under Woodford that flowers first appeared on the altar; he enhanced the decoration of the sanctuary by adding a mosaic floor and an alabaster and mosaic reredos. For communicants who wished to enrich their spiritual lives, he founded the Guild of St Peter for male members of the congregation and the Guild of St Elizabeth for women, and under his auspices the Middle Class Anglican School was established. Like Hook before him, the Vicar was concerned to bring the Anglican church to the working masses and developed the first permanent mission room by acquiring property in St Peter's Square, the genesis of the Church of the Good Shepherd. It was due to his efforts that the 22nd Church Congress met in Leeds in 1872, and a year later Dr Woodford was appointed to the see of Ely.

John Gott (1830–1906), vicar 1873–86

Born in Denison Hall, the youngest son of William Gott and grandson of Benjamin Gott, John Gott was the only one of Hook's successors who was brought up in Leeds. He was educated at Winchester and Brasenose College and was ordained in 1854 becoming a curate in Great Yarmouth and, following an invitation from the Revd Atlay, returned to Leeds in 1866 as vicar of Bramley where his High churchmanship caused not a little unease. According to Cosmo Lang, Gott 'loved Leeds down to its very smuts' and, when he was elected Vicar of Leeds in 1873, this devotion to his birthplace led to unceasing labours on behalf of both the church and his hometown. Within a year of his appointment, he organised a huge general mission, the first to be held outside London, and a second mission was to take place in 1883. His commitment to community outreach was to take several forms. Close to his heart was the founding of the Leeds Clergy School in 1876; never a learned divine, Gott's ambition for the School was to prepare Oxbridge graduates for their work as parish priests with a strong emphasis on their pastoral responsibilities. With the 'right' men around him, Gott believed a vicar might be able to transform a community and the Church's place within that community. Gott continued Hook's drive to build more Anglican churches in Leeds through a reorganised Leeds Extension Society, pledging to raise £100,000 to erect new churches in the poorer inner-city suburbs including All Souls, the Hook Memorial Church in Woodhouse. Like his predecessor, the Revd Woodford, Gott recognised that more informal church services in mission rooms, with supplementary educational and recreational activities, might act as 'nurseries' for the Parish Church. Under Gott's incumbency, the St Peter Square Mission thrived which led to the building of the Church of the Good Shepherd in 1881. New premises had also built for the Leeds Middle Class School. In addition to opening the Hook Memorial Church, a recumbent effigy of Dr Hook designed by Sir Gilbert Scott, was placed in the sanctuary of the Parish church, and in the apse behind the altar the Salviati mosaics of the Twelve Apostles were installed in memory of Joseph Tennant. It was also Gott that organised and paid for the return of the stones of the Anglo-Saxon crosses to Leeds and their erection in the Parish church.

Another aspect of Gott's mission was to repair the gap that had developed between the church and the town by involving himself in a whole host of organisations and societies, some philanthropic, others educational and cultural. He was active in the affairs of the Hospital for Women and Children and the Leeds Dispensary, played a leading role in the establishment of Leeds Girls High School and the Yorkshire College which later became the University of Leeds. On the cultural front he was a member of the Leeds Philosophical and Literary Society and the Leeds Fine Art Society. After twelve years of continuous exertions, he had a serious breakdown, and began a quieter life as Dean of Worcester. With his health improving, in 1891, he was appointed Bishop of Truro, a position he held until his death in 1906

Dr F. J. Jayne (1845–1921), vicar 1886–9

The son of a wealthy Welsh colliery owner, Francis John Jayne was educated at Rugby School and Wadham College, Oxford where he enjoyed a distinguished undergraduate career. In 1868 he was elected a Fellow of Jesus College, was ordained in 1870 and became a tutor at Keble College. Between 1879–1886 he was the Principal of St David's College, Lampeter. A High Churchman but with no pastoral experience, his election to Leeds in 1886 was a surprising one and he served for only two years before his nomination as Bishop of Chester where he remained for the next thirty years. Whilst Vicar of Leeds, he completed his predecessor's plans for the fitting up of a side chapel for celebration of Holy Communion on weekdays (now the Lady Chapel), and successfully experimented with regular monthly men's services.

Edward Stuart Talbot (1844–1934), vicar 1889–95

Edward Talbot was born and bred in aristocratic circles; both his grandfathers were peers, Lord Salisbury was a cousin, and his future wife was a member of the influential Lyttleton family. Educated at Charterhouse and Christ Church, Oxford he was ordained in 1870. At the relatively young age of 25, he was appointed the first warden of the newly opened Keble College where he remained for the next 18 years. A self-confessed Anglo-Catholic, he contributed an essay to the influential *Lux Mundi,* a book edited in 1889 by the celebrated Bishop of Oxford, Charles Gore. Whilst stressing the historical continuity of Catholicism, the essays sought to modernise Anglo-Catholicism by incorporating the findings of modern science and the pressing needs of the downtrodden masses. In the same year with no pastoral experience whatsoever he was appointed Vicar of Leeds by his cousin, the Conservative Prime Minister, Lord Salisbury. Within a year he was offered the bishopric of St Albans, an offer he refused, remaining in Leeds until 1895. Although he famously said that he was 'a Conservative but with a bad conscience', his years in the city further radicalised his opinions, arguing that the church was not just concerned with 'the individual soul …it must concern itself with economic morality of society too'. This was to manifest itself in Talbot's interest in trade unionism and his advocacy of an industrial partnership, views unpalatable to some socialists and most businessmen alike. The Vicar involved himself in some of the industrial disputes of the 1890s, most notably the Gas Workers strike of 1890 and the miners' dispute of 1893, but whilst believing that a ruthless capitalism might crush the meek, Talbot also argued that full employment would sap incentives to work. Although the intellectual tone of Talbot's sermons would probably have been above the heads of his congregation at the Parish church, there was his spirituality, sincerity and ability to bridge the gap between different social classes. Never negligent of his pastoral duties, many spoke of his personal kindness and fatherliness, and there was genuine grief when he announced that he had accepted the bishopric of Rochester; ten years later he became Bishop of Southwark and then Bishop of Winchester. Bishop Talbot never forgot his time in Leeds and was regularly in touch with the city and members of his former congregation.

E. C. S. Gibson (1848–1924), vicar 1895–1905

Edgar Charles Sumner Gibson was born into a distinguished clerical family in Hampshire and was a pupil at Charterhouse and an undergraduate at Trinity College, Oxford. Ordained 1872, his first post was to the chaplaincy of Wells Theological College and in 1876 he was invited by the Revd John Gott to become the first principal of the Leeds Clergy School. After four years in post, there developed a rift between Gott and Gibson regarding the academic nature of the curriculum and Gibson returned to Wells as its Principal. A prolific author of more than 300 published books and articles, he was appointed Vicar of Leeds in 1895 and in 1901 became honorary chaplain to Queen Victoria and following her death served as chaplain to Edward VII. He relinquished his Leeds incumbency in 1905 to become Bishop of Gloucester.

Samuel Bickersteth (1857–1937), vicar 1905–16

The Bickersteth family have served the Church of England for many generations. Sam's father was the evangelical Bishop of Exeter, his elder brother Bishop of Tokyo, another brother was associated with the Leeds Clergy School, whilst a cousin was Bishop of Ripon. Sam was born in Hampstead, educated the Merchant Taylor's School and St John's, Cambridge, graduating in 1881. He became a curate to the Revd. William Boyd Carpenter at Christ Church, Lancaster Gate, and when Boyd Carpenter was appointed Bishop of Ripon, Bickersteth served for four years as his private chaplain. For fourteen years before he came to Leeds, Bickersteth was Vicar of Lewisham. According to the *Yorkshire Post* the new vicar was 'not easy to classify according to the usual design – High or Low or Broad church'. An ardent champion of the temperance movement, foreign missions, and the voluntary principle in education, in 1909 he was appointed chaplain to the Third Battalion of the Prince of Wales Own Yorkshire Regiment, served as canon in the Ripon diocese and was a personal chaplain to George V. He left Leeds in 1916 when he was appointed a canon of Canterbury Cathedral. Bickersteth is probably best remembered now for his moving *Bickersteth War Diaries* published in 1998.

The Ecclesiological Society

The Ecclesiological Society is for all those who love churches and are interested in their fabric and furnishings, their use and conservation. The society was founded in 1879, as a successor to the Cambridge Camden Society of 1839. It has a lively programme including lectures, visits and an annual conference. Members also receive the society's publications – *Ecclesiology Today*, *Church Crawler* and the proceedings of our annual conference – as well as regular e-mail newsletters.

Membership is open to all. For further details, see the society's website, www.ecclsoc.org, or write to the Hon. Membership Secretary at the email address given overleaf.

Charity registration

The Society is a registered charity, number 210501. Its registered address, which should not be used for general correspondence, is c/o The Society of Antiquaries of London, Burlington House, Piccadilly, London W1V 0HS.

Membership subscriptions

Life member (UK only)	£300.00
Annual member (UK)	£17.50
Under 25/retired (UK)	£14.00
Extra household member at same address	£3.50
Overseas membership: please enquire.	

Contributions to *Ecclesiology Today*

The Editor is always pleased to receive articles for consideration, or ideas for possible contributions. In furtherance of the society's aims, articles should promote 'the study of the arts, architecture and liturgy of the Christian Church'.

Contributions should generally be based on fresh research, investigation or analysis, or have some topical relevance to the design, conservation or study of church buildings. Most articles are objective and factual but there is the opportunity for well-argued personal views on matters of wide interest to be put forward in our occasional 'Viewpoint' series. Articles which deal with an individual building are welcome, provided they go beyond a general account of the church to either highlight matters of wider significance or explore a particular aspect of the building in depth.

There is no formal process of peer-review, but articles will usually be sent to one or more readers with relevant knowledge or experience of the subject matter for an independent opinion. Publication may depend on making changes in response to their recommendations.

The guidelines for contributors can be obtained from the Editor (contact details overleaf).